THE STARTUP NAVIGATOR: GUIDING IDEAS INTO REALITY

"INDIA'S FIRST COMPREHENSIVE STARTUP GUIDE FOR BEGINNERS"

ADITYA RANJAN

Made with ♥ on the Notion Press Platform
www.notionpress.com

Contents

Preface

The Startup Navigator: Guiding Ideas into Reality

The Startup Navigator: Guiding Ideas into Reality is a guide for aspiring entrepreneurs who want to transform raw ideas into successful startups. The book will take a step-by-step approach to entrepreneurship, guiding readers through the unspooling of complexities involved in building a business and equipping them with tools and insights needed to move through it confidently.

The book provides a foundation, starting with the exploration of the entrepreneurial mindset and the essential factors that enable a startup ecosystem to succeed. It then guides the reader through critical stages, including business ideas refinement, strong teams building, scalable products and services creation, and the art of marketing and sales mastering. Full of practical strategies and lessons from real-life case studies, it provides actionable advice that readers can apply immediately to their ventures.

While not laying merely foundational knowledge, the book goes beyond and into the challenges each entrepreneur must endure in managing risk, failure, and changes in the environment. Then, the advanced topics will lead the reader through the landscapes of leadership, long-term growth, and meaningful social impact so that the businesses built are not only profitable but also purposeful.

A highlight of this book is that it targets some very important entrepreneurial skills that include selling, stress management, decision making, and adaptability to be done in an easy-to-learn manner. These are quite crucial both for the beginning but also for the survival within the competitive business environment.

The Startup Navigator was designed to answer the peculiar needs of the Indian startup ecosystem while holding relevance on a global level. The book fills gaps that are left unaddressed by entrepreneurship literature, making readers step forward boldly, and not out of hesitation, with clear confidence toward converting their ideas into a business that can thrive.

Whether you are setting out on your first entrepreneurial adventure or looking for something new as an experienced innovator, this book is not just a resource but an ally that you can count on. Acting like a mentor, motivator, and guide, it is your full roadmap for translating ideas into impactful and long-lasting legacies.

CHAPTER ONE

Navigating the Startup Landscape: An Introduction

Building a startup is quite like an expedition: many people dream about reaching the end destination of having their business but never actually prepare to start on the journey. You would not begin a cross-country hike without knowing your gear and having a map, for example; starting a business without understanding the most basic of its fundamentals has a peculiar way of taking you in the opposite direction.

In this chapter, the focus will be on the fundamental issues regarding a startup. A support system for the entrepreneurs will be related to investors, mentors, governmental support, and corporations. More importantly, a strong mindset—resilience, adaptability, and keeping a clear purpose—is crucial to staying alive in a competitive market as a startup. Enterprise owners and entrepreneurs realize beyond the mere action of launching a business that it may have an impact on innovation, driving growth within the economy, or creating employment opportunities.

Achieving these basics is not very difficult to be stuck upon. With the proper understanding of the fundamentals, entrepreneurs turn ideas into thriving ventures, and in return, they contribute to real-world economic growth and technological advancement.

The Startup Ecosystem

An ecosystem is fertile soil for a new innovative idea to bloom; it is a dynamic network that provides entrepreneurs with bold visions, investors ready to feed the dreams, mentors guiding them the way, and institutions offering that knowledge and tools for success. This ecosystem is not individualistic but a collective push by all the incubators, accelerators, and government agencies to nurture startups from the ground up.

Whether it is funding, mentorship, infrastructure, or market access, each adds its unique resource to the transformation of ideas into scalable businesses. All these webs of support foster innovation, drive economic growth, create jobs, and propel technological advancements.

Successful startup ecosystems thrive on collaboration, a bit of risk-taking, and the free flow of capital—the applause by entrepreneurs to challenge the status quo. You will learn about the heart of the startup ecosystem: understanding and getting familiar with all the foundational terminologies and players that make the startup world tick. Deep knowledge of how ecosystems work and what role each participant plays is vital, and so this section will equip you with more than enough information to better navigate and thrive in the startup landscape.

Entrepreneurs

Entrepreneurs are risk-takers who bring challenges around and turn them into opportunities. To others, they may only see barriers; to entrepreneurs, they see solutions. With boldness in risk-taking, innovative ideas, and lots of experimenting, entrepreneurs make great changes in industries and drive economic growth. For example, through initiatives such as Tesla and SpaceX, Elon Musk transformed the automotive and aerospace sectors by pushing boundaries at what one thought was possible. Oprah Winfrey took personal pain and made it into a global success by the innovation of a new medium, an epitaph of resilience. Steve Jobs defined the technology world with his return to Apple, especially when one takes into account the iPhone-he transformed the living essence by which we, as the human race, make our lives. Some entrepreneurs create jobs and money for people; others reshape society through innovative products. Their tenacity, enthusiasm, and drive for success, even after the cost of failure, create growth that changes markets and fuels transformation.

Investors

The investor is one of the most essential parts of the startup ecosystem, as he provides the most important fuel to go in for growth: delivering financing, resources and connections that help a business to grow and do well. For instance, in the much-watched Shark Tank, investors provide more than funding; they also provide valued mentorship and strategic guidance for entrepreneurs. Before proceeding to invest, these investors scrutinize closely and with pertinent knowledge the underlying potential for returns associated with the company, advise the entrepreneur on overcoming problems, and expand the business.

They invest in new startups that contribute to ideas, which make for economic growth and progress in the industries. Their contributions turn promising ideas into successful businesses by converting the dreams into reality with finance and expertise.

Incubators and Accelerators

These organizations provide many services to new and growing startups such as access to office spaces, advice from incubators, and access to networks in return for fees or equity. In contrast, incubators generally collaborate with startups at an earlier stage for a relatively longer period, while accelerators are short-term programs emphasizing rapid growth.

Educational Institutions

Their part includes universities and colleges that offer entrepreneurship programmes and other opportunities along with a pool of skilled graduates. They partner with startups through innovation labs, partnerships with others etc. This plays an important role for the startups started by college students in colleges as it provides office spaces, networks and investment in some cases

Government and Regulatory Bodies

The government supports ventures through its grants, tax breaks, infrastructural developments and other policies. The government regulates the environment of startups in an effort to make sure everyone has an equal opportunity; also protects intellectual property as well.

There are several programs like Startup India that provide tax exemptions and funding, while the SBIR program in the US offers grants for tech-driven research. Singapore's Enterprise Development Grant funds up to 80% of innovation projects. All these initiatives will help startups to scale up, innovate and enter new markets.

Corporate Partnerships

Corporate partnerships can be a game-changer for startups, providing access to resources, expertise and reach that takes a startup years to build. By collaborating with established companies, startups can gain valuable industry insights which can help a startup grow fast.

Spotify partnered with Hulu to offer bundled subscriptions. Through this collaboration both. companies profited and thereby granted both firms an opportunity to reach each other's customers

These partnerships give startups the drive to innovate, scale, and succeed while corporates are given fresh ideas and new markets they increasingly seek.

Why Startups Matter in Today's Economy

Startups are important, not just for the economy but also to fuel economic growth and innovation, ensure better job opportunities, and add importance to today's economies globally. Startups go way beyond small businesses in the new economy; They are the nurseries of innovation and invention of new technologies, scalable solutions, and breakthroughs that can disrupt the status quo entirely. Their innovative ability and quick adaptability allow them to respond to real-world problems emerging trends.

Driving Innovation and Technological Advancement

Startups are by nature innovators who revolutionize the boundaries of technology though innovation in new products and services. Without the corporation structure, they tend to survive in environments encouraging flexibility and ingenuity.

AI start-up NVIDIA is reputed to develop advanced solutions to complex problems. Strip and Square are examples of fintech start-up disrupting traditional banking and payment systems. CRISPR Therapeutics is a biotech start-up that pioneered gene editing technologies, while Tesla and Sunrun are at the forefront of a shift away from traditional energy sources to clean energy sources.

The most crucial factor is that startups are capable of taking risks and pivoting quickly. This creates an environment of fast-paced innovation. Agility helps them quickly respond to changes in market conditions, customer needs, and technology developments. Accordingly, the industry is constantly redescribing those firms, and new opportunities for growth and development are continually made. Startups drive economic growth and transform people's lives by embracing innovation and technological advancement.

Job Creation and Economic Development

Start-ups are an important source of employment. While massive corporations can dominate the headlines, it is start-ups and small businesses that account for the newest job creations. As these companies grow, they create jobs across industries-from software development to marketing and sales. In developing markets, studies show that start-ups tend to disproportionately participate in job growth, especially where they drive employment in sectors critical to development. This new employment ripples on from the individual, creating sustaining ripples in communities and economic growth.

Encouraging Competition and Market Disruption

Startups disrupt the status quo long-established businesses have provided. Most of the time, they give fresh concepts and new business models to the market. They implement innovative pricing, customer-centric solutions, and other means of executing product and service delivery, and that makes the bigger players conform to it or become obsolete. Healthy competition benefits consumers because quality is better, price is lower, and technology assimilation is faster. There are even newer ideas that the startups have come up with which include disruption in the transportation industry with ride-sharing and finance by peer-to-peer lending.

Fostering Globalization and Market Expansion

Due to digital platforms, e-commerce, and cloud-based technologies, today's startups can grow globally and at a speed never experienced before. International markets are thereby opened for access to new pools of consumers, interaction with global talent, and exposure of innovations to a population spread across different corners of the globe. Further, through entering international markets, startups globalize the economy, and increase cross-border trade and collaboration.

Solving Social and Environmental Challenges

Most mission-driven startups centre around pressing social and environmental issues that contribute toward positive changes in human life and the planet. Social enterprises and impact startups generally grapple with large, broad challenges of poverty, healthcare access, education, and sustainability.

As Warby Parker and TOMS have done for social responsibility; education-focused start-ups such as Coursera and edX democratize quality education; as medical delivery in hard-to-reach places is promised through Zipline and Matternet's usage of drones.

Examples include sustainable innovations with startups such as Tesla and Vestas transitioning to renewable energy, innovation of how a company like TerraCycle and Enevo handle waste and recycling, or how startups like Carbon Engineering and Climeworks seek to capture carbon emissions to mitigate climate change.

Such entrepreneurial ventures working on solution-based ventures solve social problems that orthodox businesses or governments might ignore or fail to cope with, thus making a sustainable future for our earth and enabling millions of people across the planet.

Attracting Investment and Stimulating Venture Capital

This is the most critical component of the venture capital ecosystem-startups. Investors are always on the lookout for businesses with high growth potential; hence, these businesses provide startups an opportunity to invest in such potential. All such venture capital inflows support new product development, market expansion, and talent acquisition. The quest for the next "unicorn," this funding cycle finances, accelerates economic activities in all sectors toward growth.

Building Resilient and Agile Economies

A startup ecosystem encourages economic resilience by actively engaging in adaptability and diversification. This agility allows a startup to respond flexibly to changing market dynamics, economic crisis, or to pivot when the ground beneath shifts due to changes in technology. This in turn creates a more diversified and robust economy, which is no longer reliant on one or two main industries. For example, when the COVID-19 pandemic struck, the exponential growth of startups in e-commerce, telemedicine, and all technologies for remote work was exponential, providing critical services and keeping economies moving.

Developing a Culture of Entrepreneurship

It breeds an entourage effect on the culture of entrepreneurship, as entrepreneurs inspire and motivate others into starting their ventures. The culture of entrepreneurship causes unending cycles of innovation and economic stimulation with employment opportunities everywhere. Many regions have sprouted startup ecosystems in support networks, funding opportunities, and mentorship for the coming generation of entrepreneurs.

The Entrepreneurial Mindset

This entrepreneurial mindset is a form of attitude of innovation, problem -solving and adaptation to challenges. Starting a business is not hard but having a mindset for creativity and an urge to find new opportunities makes a good entrepreneur. The right mindset is very important in this field as every step has different problems and challenges; to grow and make a successful startup we need to have a good and right mindset to tackle the challenges and to find new and best opportunities to grow.

Embracing Risk and Uncertainty

Entrepreneurs do not fear risks, they know that with the approach to starting up, some uncertainty is involved. Instead of running from it, they prepare for it and make decisions based on unknown outcomes. A correct approach is the master key to tackling any stubborn problem; doing research, planning and pivoting when necessary is a huge part of the entrepreneurial mindset as well as managing this risk intelligently.

Resilience and Perseverance

Building a startup is never easy, and failure is part of the process. Only 10 per cent of the startups achieve success and 90 per cent fail. The mind-set of an entrepreneur is to view setbacks as learning opportunities rather than giving up on such occasions. Instead of getting through difficulties, they push forward with much determination. This resilience helps them avoid giving up and keeps them moving on by changing their strategies whenever necessary.

Creative Problem-Solving

Entrepreneurs view problems as an opportunity. They are always ready to find ways that can efficiently solve a problem in a more innovative and creative manner. It pushes them to think out of the box and come up with new ideas, which ultimately makes their business stand out from others. To be on the right track in the speedy world of startups, being adaptable and finding ways to solve problems innovatively is the key to survival.

Taking Initiative

An entrepreneurial attitude is being proactive rather than waiting for things to happen. Entrepreneurs do not sit back; they make the opportunity. This also entails a self-motivated attitude and willingness to work hard, though little direction and support might be involved in the early stages of a business.

Adaptability and Flexibility

Adaptability and flexibility in a fast-changing business world are very important for entrepreneurs. Markets evolve because of changes in consumer preferences, new technology, and other global factors, like the economic crisis. Strategies change according to the inputs an entrepreneur receives regarding such market behaviour. BigBasket and Zepto are two examples wherein both service providers introduced 10- minute delivery services targeting more demand from consumers.

The risk of not following the market trends is clearly shown by failed startups such as Kodak and Blockbuster. Comparatively, companies such as Swiggy and Zomato expanded from delivering food into quick commerce, which shows the necessity for flexibility to meet changing customer needs. Of course, success lies ahead of getting a trend that leaves one ready to adapt when necessary.

Long-Term Vision

Successful entrepreneurs experience setbacks in the short run because they have a longer-term vision. A large view will keep them focus, align their teams, and continually make strategic decisions to foster sustainable growth.

For example, Jeff Bezos took Amazon from an online bookstore and grew it into one of the world's biggest tech companies focused on future diversified services such as AWS. Similarly, Musk envisioned Tesla as more than just electric cars but as part of a sustainable energy future that helped Tesla sneak past financial struggles and production matters.

Learning and Curiosity

An entrepreneurial spirit grows on continuous learning and unlimited curiosity. Entrepreneurs believe that the world is continuously changing, and one cannot be relevant if not well-informed on anything—breakthrough technologies, market dynamics, or even a shift in customer preference. The curiosity of an entrepreneur provokes them to uncover fresh insights and gain knowledge from each possible source so that the business stays competitive and progressive.

For an entrepreneur, learning is not a habit but a necessity. Every discovery, no matter how small, becomes a stepping stone for adaptation, growth, and innovation, shaping a future filled with endless possibilities.

Networking and Collaboration

No entrepreneur is successful entirely on his or her own. This is what develops the entrepreneurial mindset to realize that value lies in building a strong network of experience. These include mentors, advisors, partners, and fellow entrepreneurs who are around to learn with and from. It also opens up doors for various opportunities and resources as well as ideas, which they would otherwise not be able to gain if they tried doing things on their own.

Common Myths in Building a Startup

Many myths confuse would-be entrepreneur while launching a business. Such myths make people believe in unrealistic hopes and add more stress to them.

Here are some common myths that need to be cleared up for

anyone who wants to build a successful startup:

You Need a Perfect Idea to Start:

The biggest lie is that one needs a brilliant and innovative idea before initiating a business venture. Mainly, most of the successful companies in the world start with simple ideas, which evolve into bigger concepts over time. For example, Instagram started as an application that helped check-in, initially called Burbn but evolved to become a photograph-sharing platform because users liked the photo-sharing feature most. Your idea doesn't have to be perfect; it just needs to solve a problem and can be made better as you grow.

You Must Have a Lot of Money:

Another myth is that starting up needs a lot of money. That may be partially true, but many startups begin with small sums of money and toil hard for success. Companies like Mailchimp started with minimal outside funding and created value through the use of their own money and careful planning. It is more about using resources wisely, being cautious in spending, and finding smart ways to grow.

Overnight Success is Possible:

We hear a lot of stories about overnight success. However, most successful startups take years of persistence, hard work, and lots of learning from mistakes. Even companies such as Amazon or Airbnb needed some time to build their solid foundation. So, the idea of overnight success can be very frustrating if things do not happen overnight, but thinking for the long-term and being patient is extremely important in terms of startup success.

Failure is the End:

Many believe that a failed startup signals the end of the road. But in reality, failure is often the spark that ignites future success. History is full of stories of entrepreneurs who overcame setbacks and rose to incredible heights. For example, Ritesh Agarwal, the founder of OYO, faced multiple rejections and financial struggles during the initial phase of his business. However, he transformed those failures into improvements on his model, thus converting OYO into one of the largest hospitality chains worldwide.

Failure teaches lessons that success never can. Each setback reveals insights, highlights gaps, and paves the way for better strategies. It's not the end—it's a turning point that builds resilience and sharpens your approach. Remember, failure is a temporary detour, not the final destination on your entrepreneurial journey.

You Need to Do Everything Yourself:
Many people think that founders must do everything—be the marketers, developers, salespersons, and more—but this is not true. Startups often need to do many tasks at first, but it is important to build a strong team and ask for outside help to grow well. Find people who have different skills and don't be afraid to let others take on tasks. As your business gets bigger, working together will be important for success.

Believing in these myths can make your startup journey tougher than it really should be. Success does not result from having a perfect plan, not giving up, and learning instead, but trying to follow an almost foolproof plan. Knowing about and correcting these misunderstandings early on prepares you for a more realistic and satisfying business experience.

Case Study: Airbnb – From Idea to Disruption

Airbnb was started in 2008, when Brian Chesky, Joe Gebbia, and Nathan Blecharczyk found inspiration to help people rent out spare rooms in their homes. The idea came from seeing a chance to give travellers affordable places to stay and help homeowners make a little extra money.

The Startup Ecosystem:

When it started, Airbnb had a really rough time. However, using the core elements of the startup ecosystem-online platforms, social media for marketing, and the growing phenomenon of the sharing economy-they created a user-friendly website and app that leveraged the infrastructure of the internet to connect hosts and guests and scale the business very effectively.

Why Startups Matter in Today's Economy

Airbnb is an example of how the startups are able to replace traditional industries. The hospitality industry had enjoyed the sole monopoly with hotels, but Airbnb's innovative model scaled up its services and became a global brand, valued in hundreds of millions. This shift opened up new business opportunities and gave consumers more choice and cheaper travel.

The Entrepreneurial Mindset:

Founders worked with a lot of determination and resourcefulness in addressing the fears of the investors concerning them. They overcame some legal issues related to holding the business in various cities. They changed their strategy to focus on building a community and winning user trust. They looked at ever-changing customer feedback to improve the platform.

Key Takeaways:

- Identifying Market Gaps: Most successful startups begin with an identification of unmet needs or gaps in the market, just like Airbnb.
- Leverage Technology: They can be able to leverage technology to streamline the business and reach so many more people.
- Understand Change: It is a mindset of change and readiness, thriving in the face of setbacks.

CHAPTER TWO

Charting the Course: From Idea to Concept

Reality magic is that moment when an idea takes its actual shape in a new business. It is not just a good idea; it is also always improving it to become something useful and important. So, it begins with the development of your idea, actually making sure that it solves a problem or fulfils a need. Getting early feedback from potential users, mentors, or coworkers makes an enormous difference- it's an indication of whether the idea is doable and where you may need to change it before continuing. That helps you get started with a well-thought-through, well-defined plan, avoiding expensive mistakes later on.

Market research is quite fundamental in understanding the territory you are stepping into. Therefore, if you know who your target people are, what they want, and what your competitors have, then you can make much more informed decisions. It's like having a business-map with all the navigation skills. Without this information, you are a bit lost. Sensible market research will highlight opportunities and avoid problems, ensuring the startup stands out in a saturated marketplace.

The last part is defining your USP. This illustrates how your product or service is different and better in comparison others. It is what catches the attention, and then attracts your customers' selection of you. This chapter teaches you the tools, examples, and tactics to help you move from an idea to a business ready for the market. It's more the art of making brilliant, keen choices at each turn so that your idea blossoms into a startup that disrupts and impacts the market.

Identifying and Refining Your Idea

Ideas are the seeds from which startups grow, but having an idea is absolutely no way near half done. Idea without execution is nothing. In fact, what matters is finding a good idea and then hammering it down according to the realities of the world. A successful idea is not about creativity, but rather it embodies solving problems, giving values, and differentiation in the marketplace. There are several steps in which you can identify and refine your idea.

Step 1: Understand the Problem You're Solving

It is at the heart of every good idea- a problem. The more stressful or widespread the issue, the more potential there is for your idea to be successful. Take some time to consider what your idea is trying to solve. Is it something that impacts many, or is it a niche one that impacts a smaller set of people? Understanding this will guide how you form and position your idea.

Step 2: Get Feedback Early

Once you get the basic idea, get it out quickly for early feedback. That way, you would know whether your idea has some immediate resonance with potential users and where adjustments might be needed. Don't be afraid to share the concept with trusted friends, mentors, or even potential customers. Their insights will prove invaluable in refining your idea. You can use different types of tools to gather feedback on your startup idea which are Google Forms, SurveyMonkey, Hotjar, User Testing, Slack Communication, Usability Hub. These tools will help you to get the best insights and the feedback will be very helpful in building a startup.

Step 3: Adapt and Refine

One important thing to do when refining an idea is to be open to a change of direction. Usually, the idea does not remain the same as it was initially contemplated. Be prepared to make changes based on information received from various sectors, changes in the market, and other insights from experience over time. Flexibility will determine just how one finds a perfect fit between the idea and the market.

Step 4: Validate Your Passion

Being passionate about an idea is just as important as finding an idea that solves a problem. Building a startup is a long and arduous process; passion will drive you on those really tough days. Ask yourself if this is something you are excited to work on when things get tough. If so, then you're off to a good start.

Falguni Nayar, the founder of Nykaa, takes a simple observation and turns it into a game-changing business. As an investment banker, she was observing a huge gap in the Indian beauty market. There was limited access for consumers to quality beauty products, buying cosmetics often was inconvenient, and often uninformed. None of the platforms combined a broad range of products with some form of guidance on how to apply them effectively.

Taking the opportunity, Nayar visualized Nykaa as a one-stop shop for beauty enthusiasts, not just for selling products but also offering expert advice and educational content. She worked out her idea meticulously, focusing on authenticity, customer trust, and a seamless shopping experience. This unique approach struck the right chord with Indian consumers, who were looking for a reliable and comprehensive beauty platform.

Nykaa today stands out as one of the best success stories for a startup in India, transforming the beauty landscape. The story of Falguni Nayar speaks volumes about identifying a gap, sharpening a vision, and then bringing it into existence with passion and precision—a great lesson for any entrepreneur looking to transform ideas into reality.

Idea Validation and the Litmus Test

This is when you determine whether your idea has potential or is merely a thought. So many entrepreneurs get so caught up in the excitement of their concept that they forget to seek validation. This means that even the most exciting ideas can fall flat. Validation is important because it validates that your product or service solves a real problem, there's actual demand for it and connects with your target market. It is a reality check for you that can save you time, money, and energy as you hone up on your idea before you take the idea to the market.

This process will help you to answer the critical questions: Does this solve a problem people care about? Will they pay for it? More than just gut feeling, idea validation grounds your startup in real-world needs and eliminates the uncertainty that can sink a startup's prospects.

The litmus test is one of the most effective validation techniques for your idea, a technique you can use to check the reaction of the market toward your concept before you commit to full capacity. It's like a sneak peek into the future of your idea: Will people want what you're offering? It helps you avoid building a whole product that may not make it, and you can pivot early if necessary.

Instead of full product development, the litmus test makes you design an MVP, which stands for a Minimum Viable Product, in other words, a basic version of your idea with core features. In this way, you manage to test the market without too much investment. You share your MVP with potential customers, gather early feedback, and see if your solution is something they will buy into. If customers see value in your MVP and are interested, you're sure you are on the right track.

The best example of litmus test use is Dropbox. Instead of creating the whole platform, Dropbox's founder designed a short video to demonstrate how he would work out the tool. It generated user interest and gave him real feedback as to whether the concept was good before writing one single line of code. Dropbox saved both time and money by proving a possible idea through this early litmus test.

This can also be done from the landing page, even by pre-selling the product. The idea here is that you can track the interest or willingness to buy from your users before a full product launch. Therefore, you can then determine whether your idea is worth pursuing. You will thus know real insights about customer demand and have the opportunity to refine or change before making enormous investments.

In other words, the litmus test does not only validate your notion but it also serves as a safety net to ensure that you use your time and energy in the right direction. A good entrepreneur knows very well that it doesn't matter how well an idea is executed; it's only as good as the proof behind it and that simple litmus test is what makes the difference between a product that stays alive and a product that dies.

Conducting Market Research and Validation

Among the most important things to do in building a proper startup is market research and validation. In fact, these helps to understand the needs, behaviours, and preferences of your target audience, as well as whether your product or service solves a real problem.

Most start-ups fail due to misjudgement about the demand in the market or lack of understanding on the part of customers. Such preliminary research becomes even more crucial in countries like India, where cultural, traditional, and religious aspects have a great influence on consumer behaviour. The Indian marketplace is very sensitive when it comes to prices that consumers are most habituated to negotiating on goods and services provided. These are essential to understand to implement the perfect pricing and marketing strategies for the business. Most customers invest a lot of time finding something that is even cheaper and better, and thus these patterns need to be understood to design perfect pricing and marketing strategies.

Thorough research can help you in:

- Understanding how consumer preferences vary across different regions.
- Deal with the sensitivity of pricing Indian market.
- Position the product in a proper place about native values and cultural sensibilities

How to Conduct Market Research and Validation:

- Know your target audience: In India, for example, knowing and understanding the cultural differences between the Indian state's spending habits and regional preferences helps. Use surveys, interviews, and online tools to go out there and inquire about your audience's pain points.
- Analyse the competitors: Understand your competitors, who are working in different parts of India. What do they have to offer? How do they deal with pricing and bargaining with customers? A competitor analysis will give you a good insight into where the gaps exist and how you can make a difference in your product.
- Leverage online tools: Utilize tools such as Google Trends and social media to know what people are searching for and talking about. India's ever-increasing internet user base provides you with a tremendous opportunity to generate insight through digital means. Direct engagement is possible via Instagram and Twitter; you get instant feedback from customers about your product.
- Test with an MVP: Once you have an idea of whom you are looking for, create an MVP—a bare-bones version of your product with only core features. Now, it will allow you to test demand without heavy investment. Get word-of-mouth feedback from potential customers, particularly on pricing. Indians always look for a good value proposition and would spend enough time negotiating to get the best deal.

Why This Research Matters for a Successful Startup:

Considering the complexity of an Indian market, with regional preferences and cultural diversity being immense, it is just beneficial to conduct market research and validation as they are necessary. Appropriate research will allow you to ascertain such an opportunity, help you tailor your product to the local requirements, and formulate a marketing strategy to be used in India. Knowing the price-conscious and haggle-sensitive Indian buyers means you can position your product or service more effectively and have long-term relationships with customers.

When Bhavish Aggarwal and Ankit Bhati co-founded Ola, they knew that just replicating the Western model of ride hailing was not going to be enough for India. They did thorough market research on understanding India's price-sensitive consumers as well as what were their unique transportation needs, thus realizing that most users of transport relied on auto-rickshaws and shared taxis, thus the development of services like Ola Auto and Ola Share specifically tailored for the Indian user. Ola's dynamic pricing and frequent discounts matched the Indian psyche of bargaining and deal-seeking. Starting small, with minimal services in specific cities, Ola was able to test its demand and rapidly scale based on very real user feedback. This approach made Ola one of the most successful Indian startups, transforming urban transportation.

For any startup in a country as diverse and price-sensitive as India, conducting market research and validation is the most important thing to ensure success. It helps to understand cultural differences and consumer behaviour and to adapt prices and products according to local needs. This ensures that the seed of the startup will be rooted in actual demand in the marketplace, thus best discovering success within India's ever-changing marketplace.

Defining Your Unique Selling Proposition

Your Unique Selling Proposition (USP) is the key that sets your startup apart in a crowded marketplace. It's the distinctive factor that makes your product or service stand out from the competition. Whether it's an innovative feature, a unique customer experience, or unmatched quality, your USP becomes the compelling reason customers choose you over others.

If you're not the first player in your domain, a strong USP becomes even more critical. In a highly competitive market, differentiation is essential to grab attention and carve out a space for yourself. Your USP helps customers see the unique value your startup brings and why you're the right choice for their needs.

A well-defined USP not only attracts customers but also builds loyalty, turning them into advocates for your brand. It's not just about what you offer—it's about why it matters to your audience. Nail your USP, and you will not only survive but thrive in any competitive market.

How to Define Your USP:

- Understand What Your Target Customers Care About Most First: Focus on what your target customers care about most. What problems do they need to have solved, and what are their pain points, your USP should be distinct, where the same, likely unending sea of offerings from competitors cannot offer them what you are offering here.
- Identify Your Strengths: What does your startup do better than everyone else? Is quality superlative, affordable, with superior customer service, or does it have innovative features? It is these strengths that will be employed to craft an effective USP.

- Analyse Competitors: See what your competitors are offering and how they are positioning themselves. Look for areas where there is a gap in your area of success. This should enable you to highlight what your product uniquely offers and contributes.

In case your USP is somewhat complex, then simplify it for your customer. Be sure that you communicate the essence of what sets your product or service apart quickly, and why it is better.

Define your USP clearly to stand out from the competitive marketplace, develop commitment and trust from your customers, and drive growth for your business.

The USP of Zomato is that it combines convenience, variety, and reliability together. It has a hyper-local approach that ensures food delivery in under 30 minutes to a very wide range of cuisines from nearby restaurants. Its real-time tracking and verified user reviews make it a trustworthy experience for foodies, and exclusive features such as Zomato Gold bring unmatched savings for the regular customer. It is not just food delivery but an all-in-one dining companion.

Case Study: Ola – From Idea to Nationwide Success

Founded in 2010 by Ankit Bhati and Bhavish Aggarwal, Ola changed the face of transportation in urban India. From being an answer to Bhavish's frustration with hiring a car to move around town, it quickly transformed into one of the largest ride-hailing platforms in India, focusing on cabs, auto-rickshaws, bike rides, and shared rides.

Identification and Idea Development

Ola initially targeted car rentals but soon understood that the company's founders needed a more accessible, flexible, and affordable transport solution. Refining that, Ola then moved into a ride-hailing platform to meet the unique needs of the Indian commuter: filling in the gap in the market for a reliable urban transport system.

Idea Validation and Litmus Test:

Ola's litmus test was straightforward: they tested demand in certain cities with some cabs. The response was overwhelmingly positive, especially when supported by dynamic pricing and deals that resonated well within India's price-sensitive culture. This validated their hypothesis about the demand to scale up services rather than trumpeting it.

Market Research and Validation:

This was largely driven by market research, which reflected the need for affordable yet unique modes of transportation such as auto-rickshaws and ridesharing services. Therefore, Ola created - Ola Auto and Ola Share to give hundreds of millions of Indians a service that meets their day-to-day needs. They also soon realized that to cover most of the market, they needed to accept cash payments.

Creating Your Unique Selling Proposition:

Their USP was providing affordable options from auto-rickshaws to cabs under one platform. Ola placed its unique focus on India's special requirements: affordability, flexibility, and localized services. This is the reason why Indian needs have found a perfect fit in Ola.

Ola's story is the best example of refining an idea, testing it with a market, and responding to the needs of a local market through research. Making use of and then supporting the identification and validation of specific transportation needs in India, Ola built a service that strongly resonated with customers, hence its place as one of the most successful startups in India.

CHAPTER THREE

Building the Vessel: Assembling the Team and Resources

A startup is a ship to be built. It is a vessel that travels through some of the roughest, most unpredictable waters imaginable; such a vessel needs a good foundation and sufficient resources to ensure weathering all storms. A startup's heart resides within its core team's variety of skills, shared vision, and commitment without it, the idea will not come alive. The journey begins with choosing the right co-founder and early team members who bring technical, operational, or strategic expertise to the startup. A well-balanced blend of expertise is critical for agility and growth in a startup. Another important element of the ecosystem is a collaborative culture, which allows room for innovation and problem-solving, where the members have an emotional investment in the startup's mission.

But a good team is not enough -- strategic resource management goes hand in hand. Whether bootstrapped, via angel investors or financed by venture capital, attaining initial funding provides that fuel to get the venture off the ground. There are the right tools, technology, and appropriate workspace, be it physical or virtual, that enables them to work efficiently, ideate freely, and then drive innovation forward. These resources should be managed sensibly, only then a startup functions smoothly, overcomes problem after problem, and caters to market demands.

Finding Co-Founders and a Great Team

Any startup requires a good team rather than a group of individuals; the team is the pillar of the whole venture. A good team for the startup provides stability, support, and adaptability, helping the startup thrive and grow. The most critical aspect is finding the right co-founder; they are not only partners but also individuals who have complementary skills, a shared vision, and an unwavering commitment to making the idea work. For instance, one co-founder might be the creative mind and technical lead, and another could focus on managing the business or handling marketing, balancing the company's foundation. Such diverse skills enable co-founders to fill in each other's gaps as they address a massive area of challenges in building a startup.

Assembling a committed team is more than just having the right co-founders; it is about gathering talented individuals who share your vision and drive. A good team acts as a force multiplier where every member brings unique skills and perspectives to the table. Early hires often wear multiple hats, matching the founders' energy and showing resilience by tackling challenges head-on with creativity and determination.

Such a shared sense of purpose breeds a collaborative and dynamic workplace where everyone is working together toward the same objectives. Together, such a team not only overcomes failures but also propels the startup forward, laying down long-term growth and success foundations.

How to Find the Right Co-Founder and Build a Great Team:

1. Qualitative attributes to look for in a co-founder and team members:

- Complementary Skills: For co-founders, look for someone whose skills balance yours. If you're a tech expert, seek someone skilled in business, finance, or marketing. Similarly, for team members, each person should bring in a specific skill set that adds value to the startup, such as product development, customer relations, or operations.
- Alignment of Vision and Values: A co-founder and team must share a common vision for the startup's mission and core values. This unity of purpose keeps everyone motivated and committed, especially when challenges arise.
- Adaptability and Resilience: Startups are full of uncertainties, so look for individuals who are flexible, open to feedback, and able to pivot when necessary.
- Passion and Commitment: Early team members should believe in the mission as strongly as the founders. They should be invested in the company's growth and feel like stakeholders, not just employees.

2. Where and How to Find the Right People:

- Network in relevant circles: Attend industry events, startup meetups, and workshops where you can connect with like-minded professionals and potential co-founders. Often, the best partnerships come from shared interests and goals within the industry.
- Start with your Network: Talk to trusted contacts who understand your values and goals. They may refer talented individuals who would be a good fit for the startup's mission and

culture.

- Utilize Online Platforms: LinkedIn and AngelList are great places to find people with specific skills interested in the startup world. Many professionals here are open to innovation and new opportunities.
- Prioritize culture fit: When recruiting, ensure that the person's values can go in line with your mission and culture. Skills are important, but a shared commitment and collaborative spirit are what makes a team cohesive and resilient.

Co-founder of MobiKwik, Upasana Taku knew that building a good team is more important than having just a great idea for building a successful fintech platform. She and Bipin Preet Singh launched MobiKwik in 2009 with a mission to simplify digital payments in India. Upasana focused on building a team with diverse expertise from technology to customer engagement to achieve this mission.

This collective effort has helped MobiKwik to present a secure and user-friendly platform that easily found itself in the competitive market of fintech. The journey of Upasana highlights that a strong, skilled team is necessary to execute ambitious ideas and drive a startup towards success.

Building a successful startup requires a team that act as the pillars of the venture. With a balanced and dedicated co-founding team and early members who bring skills and passion, a startup gains the strength and flexibility it needs to grow. Identifying people who share the vision, are resilient, and complement one another's abilities is critical to this process. When you build a team that's aligned with the mission and has the skills to bring it to life, you're setting up a foundation strong enough to take on challenges, scale effectively, and bring bold ideas into reality.

Establishing roles, responsibilities and culture

In a startup, roles, responsibilities, and culture go beyond organizational structure. They form the backbone of clarity, efficiency, and growth. In the early days, when team members juggle multiple tasks, defining clear roles ensures everyone understands their purpose and avoids confusion or overlap. With clearly assigned responsibilities, each individual knows how their efforts align with the larger mission of the company, fostering accountability and focus.

This structure gives a sense of unity where each piece fits perfectly into the bigger picture. A well-defined framework not only streamlines operations but also builds a collaborative environment where team members work in harmony with each other and drive the startup forward with purpose and energy.

Defined startup culture is your compass, directing how to work, communicate, or address the given problems by your team. Such a culture, built on innovation, respect, and resilience, brings the team together to push through difficult times and find creative solutions. A strong culture doesn't just guide how work is done; it motivates the team to support each other and align with the startup's vision, setting the basis for trust and loyalty truly invaluable while the company scales.

Clear roles and responsibilities are powerful tools for growth. They allow each team member to specialize and dive deeply into their tasks, fostering expertise and accelerating skill-building. Defined roles create space for team members to excel in their areas without stepping on each other's toes, making decision-making faster and more effective. This clarity not only drives productivity but also instils confidence, enabling everyone to contribute their best toward the startup's goals.

Think of Paytm at the start. When digital wallet services started gaining momentum, it was very clear about who did what, and one of the co-founders handled the product development ensuring all the technology and user experience was good while others managed partnerships and financial strategy. It all worked out pretty clearly to have all aspects of the business well-managed, offering room for rapid growth. The startup culture is innovation-oriented with customer-centric solutions and a unifying force for the team towards the goal of access to digital payments in India.

A startup's culture drives motivation and glues the team together by leading over the project of barriers. Open communication, creativity, and resilience are values that can help a team overcome obstacles together. When each member genuinely connects with the company mission, he's bound to bring his best and participate in the journey of the startup.

A startup with defined roles, responsibilities, and a supportive culture can manage to build a productive and motivated team. Once they have this framework in position, the team is driven to innovate, make strategically confident decisions, and make the startup sail toward prosperity in the long run.

Getting Initial Funding: Bootstrapping, Angels, and Venture Capital

Securing initial funding is vital to startups as it will act as the fuel for making ideas come into existence. Startups can source their capital through different methods; each method has different advantages:

- Bootstrapping: Bootstrapping entails using personal savings or initial sales revenue. This keeps the founders fully in charge of the business, although it can constrain rapid growth if resources become too taut.

- Angel Investors: Angels are individual investors who provide early-stage capital in exchange for equity. Often entrepreneurs themselves can offer mentorship in addition to funding, taking a start-up to a certain level before further substantial investments.
- Venture Capital: Where organizations spend large sums of money on start-ups with secured prospects, usually in the form of equity and strategic input. Investments are typically done in growth-staged start-ups that have generated traction for an idea or product.

Seed funding is normally the first capital raised in developing and testing the concept of a startup. These can come from angels, family, friends, or crowdfunding and are meant to cover critical expenses like product development and marketing. The grants that are given out by government or industry organizations offer non-repayable funds and thus form a very attractive option for those meeting specific criteria.

Funding at the early stages is important because startups can now cover essential costs: product development, hiring, and marketing. This funding allows a startup to operate, test, and refine its product, which provides it with that much-needed boost to reach customers and attract future investments.

So, here I am giving you some ways how you can secure your first funding:

- Network Strategically: Connect with industry professionals, attend events, and engage with other founders to build a network of potential investors.

- Create a Compelling Pitch: Describe the problem your startup solves, the market opportunity, and how your product stands out.
- Discuss Crowdfunding: Including Kickstarter, where start-up companies can test their ideas and solicit small donations from interested supporters.
- Accelerator programs, like Y Combinator, mobilize funding, mentorship, and resources for fast-growing start-ups to generate faster scaling and visibility.

You will have better understanding with these two examples:
One such excellent example of bootstrapping is that of Zerodha, which is India's largest stock brokerage. In 2010, Nithin Kamath and his brother began the project on personal savings without any funding. Zerodha focused on a low-cost trading platform to the Indian customers while keeping operations lean and focusing on the needs of the customers along with sound financial management. This rapid growth has been achieved in the company without external funding. Today, as the country's most profitable stockbroker, he shows that a properly applied bootstrapped strategy is not only sustainable but scalable, too.

Swiggy is the popular food delivery platform in India that pursued the other route with venture capital financing to rapidly scale. After its launch in 2014, Swiggy received its first institutional round of funding from Accel Partners and shortly gained global investors' interest.

This venture capital helped Swiggy establish a large delivery network, provide competitive discounts, and reach customers in every nook and corner of India. Using external funding, Swiggy quickly scaled its operations to become a household name and market leader in the Indian food delivery market.

These examples show the flexibility of funding approaches careful bootstrapping behind Zerodha's success, venture capital financing for Swiggy enabling rapid growth and market penetration. Both examples show the path toward long-term success based on the right kind of funding choice, made in harmony with the startups' goals.

Legal Essentials: Structuring Your Startup

Legally structuring a start-up is the key toward creating a robust, lasting foundation that supports long-term growth and protects the business. The chosen legal structure impacts nearly everything about the company-from taxes and operational rules to your personal liability and investor interest, for instance. Popularly available options in India for a start-up include: Sole Proprietorship; Partnership; Limited Liability Partnership (LLP); or Private Limited Company. All these structures have unique benefits, levels of protection, and compliance requirements that make it important to choose the one that best suits your startup goals.

This ensures that the founders' assets are not taken as part of business liability, meaning they will not be seized if a startup runs into financial or legal problems. For example, sole proprietorships are easy to form but expose the founders to unlimited personal liability. LLPs and Private Limited Companies protect the limited liability shield that protects personal assets, hence preferred for startups with more growth prospects or seeking funding. These are often preferred by startups to quickly scale up or raise investors as equity, governance, and shareholder rights have well-defined structures in Private Limited Companies.

It is the right legal structure that shall give a solid building block to set out your startup according to the connected objectives and maintain smooth operation as the company scales. Legal clarity prevents misunderstanding or potential conflict by making sure that each member appreciates their role, rights, and responsibilities. It boosts confidence among stakeholders, employees, and investors as everybody is aligned with the company's mission.

The right structure of the business right from day one minimizes risks about tax obligations or regulatory compliance. Legal structures have varied tax considerations, and one that can balance the startup's finances and possibly reduce costs about operations will be handy. For example, among LLPs and Private Ltd. Companies, startups do not mix their bank accounts with their business counterparts and, therefore, making income assessment of the companies straightforward. The defined structure will help the up-and-coming startup, and growth and scaling can easily be carried out.
Steps to Structuring Your Startup:

- Define Your Requirements and Objectives: Understand the size of your company, projected revenue, issues of liability, and intentions for growth. If growth is going to happen rapidly or investors are attracted, LLPs or private limited companies will be much more suitable options because ownership is clear and liabilities are limited.
- Register the business: Registration with the MCA in India is significant as it makes your business legitimate. It involves choosing an exclusive business name, paperwork, and filing forms to establish the company in the books of the ROC. It shows the legitimacy and trustworthiness to the stakeholders and customers alike.
- Draft of Important Papers: Private Limited Companies and LLPs have a few legal documents, which are the Memorandum of Association (MoA) and Articles of Association (AoA). All of the company's objectives, the ownership structure, and operational

rules that are in place within the company govern everyday activities and the processes to decide on anything.

- Obtain Licenses and Permits: Depending on the sector of business, some licenses may be mandatory for conducting business legally. These may be GST registration, environmental permits, or sector-specific licenses. All the required licenses help a business remain compliant without legal hassles.
- Establish Contracts: Clarity and Protection. This ensures such a relationship by an employee, vendor, or partner cannot be in place if there is no enforceable contract that shows expectations, responsibilities, and how the conflict can be resolved to ensure complete stability; avoid disputes, and safeguard intellectual property and other resources.

Case Study: Paytm - Transforming Digital Payments in India

Paytm was founded by Vijay Shekhar Sharma in the year 2010. It started with its primary services being mobile recharge and bill payments. Over time, the company has expanded to become a completely comprehensive digital payments ecosystem, offering everything from mobile wallets to financial services and changing the way Indians transact online.

Finding Co-founders and Building a Great Team:

He started Paytm single-handedly but realized pretty soon that he needed to surround himself with expertly skilled people if he wanted to scale his vision. Hence, he brought in technology, marketing, and operations experts to catapult the business forward. A diverse skill set and a shared belief in digital payments convinced Paytm to further its growth at a rapid pace.

Roles, Responsibilities, and Culture:
As Paytm keeps on growing, the need for defined roles increases. This helped the company in handling its manifold expansion. Sharma ensured that an innovative ownership and initiative-culture-driven work environment empowered employees to think outside of the box.

The hacker culture within Paytm encouraged quick decision-making and creative problem solutions, thus enabling a rapid push for launching new services at the demand of the market.

Bootstrapping, Angels, and Venture Capital:
First round of funding Paytm bootstrapped its operational startup. However, the vision attracted early-stage investors. Alibaba Group, SoftBank, and some major players funded Paytm in multiple rounds in scaling its services, and then scaling user bases.

Heavy funding came in for Paytm in 2015, when Ant Financial of Alibaba invested $680 million, catapulting the company to the big league of digital payments.

Legal Needs and Legal structuring of your startup:
The scale at which Paytm expanded its financial services threw up different legality issues. Sharma ensured that Paytm strictly followed legal compliance from banking licenses to data protection laws.

For example, to provide its wallet service, Paytm received a license from the Reserve Bank of India; the license legitimized the offering of Paytm and increased confidence among its customers. Such is the story of the success of Paytm, how a clear vision with a skilled team, strategic funding, and proper legal foundations can transform an idea into a market leader. Beyond all these, Vijay Shekhar Sharma's ability to put together the right resources and the right team at every stage has transformed a recharge platform into one of the leading digital payment companies in India.

CHAPTER FOUR

SETTING SAIL: DEVELOPING YOUR PRODUCT OR SERVICE

After you have narrowed down your idea and put together the right team, the most important thing is of-course, to create a real product or service out of that concept. This is the phase where your startup begins to take shape. Your vision starts to materialize, and it is that thumping exciting yet challenging aspect of the journey, where creativity meets practicality. Whether building a tangible product or offering a service, the ultimate goal is to solve real problems, deliver value to the customer, and ultimately resonate with them.

At this stage, you will concentrate on prototyping and building your MVP. An MVP is the minimum product having the basic features that a customer requires. Instead of jumping into a full-fledged launch, here's the opportunity to test the product with user feedback while iterating. This phase of product development will involve those decisions on balancing innovation with practicality, ensuring the solution is scalable and ready for growth.

A well-considered development would certainly set a great and sound foundation for your startup to sail into the competitive market with hopefully more chances of driving towards success.

Creating a Minimum Viable Product (MVP)

A Minimum Viable Product, or MVP, is, quite simply, the least complicated iteration of the product that would have just enough features to attract early users and validate a business idea. Instead of investing that time and resources into building a fully developed product, the MVP lets startups test the core idea at minimal cost and effort.

An MVP focuses on the essentials—the features that directly solve the problem you're targeting. Think of it as a sneak peek into what your final product could become. It's not about perfection; it's about testing the waters. By launching an MVP, you'll gather real-world feedback that reveals if people want what you're offering, how they're interacting with it, and what changes or improvements would make it even better.

Why an MVP is a Game-Changer for Startups:

- Cost-Effective Testing: A whole product would consume time, money, and resources. By developing an MVP, you can validate your idea with minimal expenses. This is particularly valuable for startups, which often have small resources.
- Speed to Market: MVP lets you get out a product quickly, get it in users' hands, and gather feedback on that product. It not only gets your product into the customer's pockets and hands faster but also lets you get ahead of the competition with improvements based on real data rather than assumptions.

- Insight into customer needs: The MVP process centres on the feedback of the user. The feedback you get provides an insight into what matters to your customers, thus allowing you to effectively build a product that would work for them.
- Reduces Risk: Creating a feature-rich product without validated user hypothesis may be a significant risk. The MVP allows you to test your hypothesis early, thereby avoiding costly mistakes by validating or killing the idea with actual users before going all in.
- Selling to Investors: An MVP with market traction becomes a powerful tool to attract funding. When investors see a product with real user engagement, it demonstrates that the concept is more than just an idea—it's a validated solution with potential. Investors are far more likely to back a startup that has taken steps to test its market appeal and shown early success, as it reduces their risk and increases confidence in the product's future.

Blueprint for Developing a Winning MVP:

Creating an MVP is about building a focused, impactful version of your product that gets to the heart of what customers need. Here's a streamlined approach to developing an MVP that brings value and momentum to your startup.

Step 1: Zero-In on the Core Problem

- Identify the Key Problem: Define what problem your product is going to solve. The key takeaway for a successful MVP is being laser-focused on solving one very specific problem for a particular audience.
- Make the Solution Simple: The solution must deliver value instantly with minimal over-complication. Your MVP should be directly attacking the core problem.

For example, the primary problem for a food delivery app may be "quick and hassle-free access to restaurants near you". The MVP solution would thus be enabling restaurant viewing near you, adding items to a cart, and ordering it.

Step 2: Select Essential Features Only

- Focus on the Bare Essentials: Only the features that are utterly necessary to solve the core problem, nothing more. Don't include "nice-to-haves" as those can come later.
- Simplify the User Experience: Make it incredibly easy to use an MVP. Design this with simplicity and functionality so users can achieve the main task without hassle.

For example, the food delivery MVP would be minimum viable with a primitive restaurant list to order, place an order, and checkout. Later advanced features such as user accounts or recommendations can be added as long as they do not outshine the main purpose.

Step 3: Launch Quickly and Gather Feedback:

- Release to Early Adopters: Push your MVP to a small set of users from whom you can gain more valuable insights. Early adopters are super useful for determining some new insights into your product.
- Collect and Refine: Use feedback toward identifying pain points or features to be added and, using the core solution as the priority, start prioritizing improvements.

For the MVP of food delivery, gather some feedback regarding order placement, user-friendliness, and overall satisfaction. Addressing the highest-impact suggestions first, you will start to get toward creating a better user experience with each iteration.

A great MVP is all about understanding those needs, focusing on what matters to users, and building a solution that could talk directly to them. It is done by breaking down your product into its core purpose to get a solution to real users as early as possible. An MVP is not about launching something perfect but getting a product into the hands of real users as soon as possible. From there, the feedback loop starts—user insights will reveal what works, what needs tweaking, and which new features could elevate the experience.

This user-centred, feedback-driven approach makes your MVP more than a test product; it turns into a dynamic foundation for growth. Every update formed by real-world interactions will bring you closer to refining and making the product ready for the market. Instead of leaving everything to assumptions, you're taking graduated, verified steps toward a solution that, for your audience, means something and evolves with your increasing understanding. And not just building a product, but building a product that's primed for impact and well-positioned for long-term success.

Prototyping, Testing, and Iterating

Prototyping, testing, and iteration are the most powerful cycles in turning ideas into life. What started with prototyping was to develop a very basic version of the product where only the core functionalities required to solve the main problem for the user would be implemented. It is not perfect but a working model designed to give you a tangible preview of your idea. By stripping down the product to its core, you provide a version of your product that is fast and cheap to build and which allows testing of the concept with minimal risk.

Testing is where you put your prototype in the hands of real users, ideally representing your target audience. This is how you'll directly gain insight into how users interact with your product, finding out what they like, what's confusing them, and what additional features they might want. Collect feedback here, so ask pointed questions, like, "What part of this product was most helpful?" or "Where did you run into trouble?"

Watch how users interact to discern what lies hidden and sometimes surprises you about people's actual behaviours during real sessions with your product. Testing serves not just to validate your assumptions but also often reveals new insights that could inform the next iteration of your product.

Then comes the continuous improvement process that brings the prototype closer to a market-ready product. You make targeted adjustments using feedback from testing to enhance the product's usability, functionality, and appeal. This is the step where your product grows, based on the real lessons learned rather than assumptions. Iteration is not something that you do once, it is a cycle. Each refactored version is then tested again, gathering new feedback and revealing new areas for improvement. In this way, your product can be aligned with real user needs, making it even more relevant, useful, and desirable at every round.

Let us now look into the journey of Zomato, which began as a simple aggregator of menus where users could browse through the menus of local restaurants. The team at the company soon realized, through several consecutive testing and iteration cycles, that there was a rising tide of demand for online ordering of food and adapted its product with order and delivery. Today, Zomato is among the leaders in food delivery in India, always iterating to meet new requirements and continue to be in the game. Having embraced the cycle of prototyping, testing, and iterating, they emerged from the basic idea into a well-cherished service.

It should be a low-risk framework for building a product that genuinely resonates with people through prototyping, testing, and iterating. Constantly refining your product based on feedback from people will not only improve it but also ensure that it is in line with what people need and want. It keeps you agile, avoids costly mistakes, and positions your product well for growth. In short, it proves that the right product isn't built by guessing but by listening, adapting, and evolving with every new insight that comes your way.

Product Development Lifecycle: From Concept to Launch

A journey from an initial idea to a fully developed product takes many stages, and all of these stages contribute heavily to the success of your startup. This method, referred to as the Product Development Lifecycle, helps in making sure that your product progresses in an organized way from abstract ideas to tangible and valuable outputs for your customers.

Conceptualization: Conceptualization marks the very beginning of an idea—the spark that sets everything into motion. It's the process of brainstorming, identifying a problem, and envisioning a practical solution. At this stage, you define the core of your product: what it is, who it's for, and how it addresses the challenges of your target market. Conceptualization isn't just about generating ideas; it's about giving them direction, purpose, and a foundation for further development.

Design and Prototyping: A well-architected concept leads to designing the product, and so the actual product is created in the form of prototypes, mock-ups or wireframes. This prototype allows experimenting with ideas concerning the features, look, and feel of the product.

Development: After testing and refining the prototype, the product goes into development. This is the phase in which your team builds the actual product-including software or manufacturing a physical item. Development involves coding, manufacturing, or assembling components, and is typically ensuring that the product functions as developed.

Testing: Testing is the most critical phase of the product development lifecycle, as this bridges the gap between development and launch. It evaluates the product thoroughly to identify bugs and usability concerns, which would ensure that it delivers the desired value to the target audience. The types of testing are :

- Alpha Testing: Conducted by the development team, alpha testing focuses on identifying critical bugs well before handing them over to external users. It gives good time for correction and smoothening.
- Beta Testing: Post the alpha test, the software product is subjected to beta testing. At this stage, it is delivered to a few, targeted external users. This captures real usability and performance feedback which indicates any outstanding issues.
- Usability Testing: This is a test for how user-friendly the product is, designed with ease of use. Real users will interact with the product to point out pain points and make sure that the product delivers according to user expectations.
- Performance Testing: This addresses how well the product performs when circumstances change. It tries to test and deliver speed, responsiveness, and stability in order to test if the product can hold its head high enough when it comes to the expected loads.

- Security Testing: This is one kind of necessary testing that is used to uncover vulnerabilities with which the product has a take on defence against certain kinds of attacks and data breaches.
- Regression Testing: It will make sure that the new code does not affect the already existing features. The functionalities already tested will work after the changes and updates.
- Acceptance Testing: This is performed by the end-users, as acceptance testing ensures that it is completely business-ready for deployment. In this final check, it is confirmed to be user-needs-friendly and matches users' expectations.

Launch: Following the proof of concept and testing and iteration, the product is now ready to go for a launch. At this stage, the product is exposed to the market by marketing, sales strategies, and getting in touch with potential users. After the launch, continuous monitoring and improvement form the core with the help of user feedback that always contributes to the evolution of the product.

A very successful product development lifecycle is Tesla's Model S. Here, Elon Musk and his team began with the concept of developing a completely electric vehicle that could be far superior to traditional cars. The result of years of research and development along with prototypes of the Model S produced identified improvements during testing, including critical design elements such as battery performance and safety features. After many generations, the Tesla Model S finally reached the shelves in 2012. This car was a new benchmark for electric vehicles and stood as an undisputed leader in the electric vehicle market.

This case highlights the importance of moving step by step through every stage of the product lifecycle. Like Tesla, a good product often requires careful development at each stage, always keeping customer convenience in mind.

Protecting Intellectual Property: Safeguarding Your Innovations

Today, as fast-paced as this world is; a startup must protect its intellectual property. Ideas and inventions are among the precious products you will create as an entrepreneur along with branding and identity. Therefore, the question is, why is IP protection essential, let us have a look at the various reasons why it matters and how best to secure it.

Why Protect Intellectual Property

Competitive Advantage: IP protection puts you ahead in the market, where unique ideas can only be yours and can never be duplicated by competitors.

Investor Attraction: A well-knit IP portfolio gives sound value to your startup and is more attractive to investors who are looking for business ventures that take care of innovation and protect their innovations.

Revenue generation: IP can be licensed or partnered to create other revenue avenues without compromising your creations.

Building Brand Trust: This safeguard of trademark and copyright strengthens brand integrity, thus promising customers to get the real thing.

Types of Intellectual Property Protection

Patents:
Patents are granted on inventions and processes, giving exclusive rights for about 20 years. The application for a patent is very detailed, demonstrating the uniqueness of the invention.

Trademarks:
Trademarks protect a name, logo, or slogan that helps your customers identify your products. A trademark cannot be used by others; otherwise, they would have to first register it.

Copyrights:
Copyrights protect the uniqueness of works by giving the creators the exclusive rights to reproduce and distribute them. These works include writings, music, art, as well as other software.

Trade Secrets:
Trade secrets are business information that is not public, giving a company an edge over others. This could be formulas or processes for something and remain a secret.

Actions towards Intellectual Property Protection:
IP Audit: Identify what needs to be protected- inventions, branding, and confidential information.

IP Registration: Patent, trademark, or copyright registration should be done based on need. If your intellectual property seems complicated or you don't know how to start the process, then seek advice from an IP lawyer.

Use Non-Disclosure Agreements (NDAs): NDAs can be used when sharing sensitive information that needs to be kept confidential.

Monitor and Enforce Your Rights: Be vigilant for unauthorized use of your IP and enforce your rights should infringement occur.

Educate Your Team: Educate your employees about the importance of IP protection and their responsibility in asset protection.

By securing those innovations with IP protection, you can protect those new ideas and be successful in this constantly competitive world of startups.

Case Study: Dropbox – Building a Global Product Through an MVP and Iterative Development

Dropbox was invented in 2007 by Drew Houston and Arash Ferdowsi to bridge the common problem of how easy it is to store and access files on several devices. After realizing that the attachments of huge files through emails were inefficient, the founders created a cloud-based system for storing files. Now, the world of cloud storage and collaboration is dominated by Dropbox with millions of users worldwide.

Creating a Minimum Viable Product (MVP)

Dropbox also began its journey through a Minimum Viable Product before building the whole product. Drop Box did not invest much in developing a fully featured system but rather made a simple demo video that indicates how the product will work. It will explain the concept of keeping files in the cloud and how the client can access his data whenever he wishes. This MVP approach allowed the founders to gauge interest without building the whole infrastructure.

The campaign went viral with thousands of sign-ups from interested users. Apart from that, Dropbox validated its concept by showing it simply. It attracted investors because it showed that this product has real market demand.

Prototyping, Testing, and Iterating

Dropbox validated the concept through the MVP and then headed into prototyping and testing. Unlike launching a full product, Dropbox built a minimum prototype to allow for uploading, storing, and syncing files across devices. It then opened up the platform to a small set of users for beta testing and gained valuable insights into usability, performance, and what's necessary.

Dropbox executed this response through relentless iteration, offering shared folders, allowing users to access data when there was no connection to the internet, and enhancing synchronization as users pointed out pain points and needs in the system. Such an iterative process gave the company the latitude to slowly develop the product without over-stretched resources or risking a major failure in launching the product.

By continuously iterating on the product and listening to the users, Dropbox ensured a well-refined, dependable product upon mass release.

Product Development Lifecycle: From Concept to Launch

Dropbox defined its product development lifecycle from the concept to a prototype and then eventually a large-scale launch. Finally, after developing the product to an extent of extensive testing, iterated, and getting everything right, Dropbox was ready for a broader release. Having successfully developed the MVP and then released it into beta testing, the company released its cloud storage solution open for mass users who could both access the free tier and pay for a premium storage tier.

Careful management of the product development lifecycle has reduced risks and increased user engagement with the product. A careful approach to development enabled Dropbox to roll out an established, scalable product to support millions of users.

A seamless transition from concept to launch helped Dropbox scale quickly and become one of the best-known names in cloud storage.

Protecting Intellectual Property: Safeguarding Your Innovations

Dropbox realized the importance of safeguarding its innovative technology. They patented cloud storage technology starting from the very beginning, which offered innovation protection and made the service more appealing to investors and partners. Additionally, they ensured that data encryption protocols were robust and that files for the users were safely protected, so confidence in their platform grew.

Protecting as much intellectual property as it could as early as possible would enable Dropbox to prevent competition from attempting to compete against the unique technology and business model Dropbox created for itself, thus realizing a great advantage in the market.

Key Takeaways

- Start Small with an MVP: Dropbox started with a simple demo video that allowed the idea to be validated without heavy upfront investments.
- Iterative Development: During the development process, listening to user feedback and continuously improving the product ensured that Dropbox meets the needs of the growing user base.
- The Structured Product Lifecycle: From idea to launch in stages helped Dropbox be able to establish the level of exposure of the product through the phases and deliver quality.
- Protecting your IP: Securing patents and data protection allowed Dropbox to scale without fear of imitation

CHAPTER FIVE

Navigating Market Waters: Marketing and Sales Strategies

Creating a new product is just the first part of your startup journey; it is getting the right customers to have the product that could determine its place in the competitive landscape. This chapter provides information on marketing and sales strategies you will apply while moving through the competitive landscape. For a new business, it becomes absolutely important how to form a robust brand identity and appropriately execute the right strategy when looking to pick up some momentum, and for an established startup seeking to scale, knowing how to create a successful brand identity and implement a solid strategy is key.

We are going to begin by defining your brand, what it stands for, and how you should resonate with your target audience. From there, it goes into the details of setting clear strategic missions and building a marketing plan that drives growth. Some essential techniques and channels for acquiring customers will also be introduced in the chapter. Lastly, you will come across proven sales strategies that will help you clinch a deal and ensure you forge deep relationships with your clients that translate prospects into permanent customers. Whether you just enter the market or expand, this chapter gives you the ultimate action insight on being successful.

Crafting Your Brand Identity

Your brand identity isn't only your logo or tagline; it is the personality of your business. It is essentially what you stand for, what values you maintain, and how you want to be seen in the marketplace. A strong brand identity builds trust, helps differentiate you from your competition, and gives people an emotional hook to connect with your audience. Its creation requires intimately knowing the target market and the message you want to project.

Defining the mission, core values, visual elements such as the logo, colours, and fonts, and even the tone of communication in marketing marks the process involved. All your brand elements have to be consistent and easily recognizable across all platforms-from your website to social media to direct customer interactions.

Vineeta Singh, the founder of Sugar Cosmetics, is the masterclass in creating a brand that truly resonates with its audience. When she started Sugar Cosmetics, it was not just selling makeup; it was about creating a bold, empowering brand that spoke directly to the millennials. She realized that conventional beauty brands catered to the very traditional ideals and saw an opportunity in breaking that market by offering products that celebrated individuality and self-expression.

From packaging to product names to marketing campaigns, everything about Sugar Cosmetics reflects confidence, fun, and authenticity. Unapologetic individuality is what the brand messaging advocates, which is why young consumers find it to be an all-time favourite since authenticity and creativity are so vital to them. Through embracing bold colours, playful content, and relatable storytelling, Vineeta built a brand identity that shone bright in a crowded beauty market.

The success of Sugar Cosmetics shows an important lesson: a good brand identity is not about logos and colours; it is more about the personality that appeals to your target audience. The journey of Vineeta Singh proves how understanding your audience and sticking to your vision can create a brand that sells not just products but inspires loyalty and love from its customers.

Strategy: Setting Strategic Missions and Plan

A strategic mission, just like plotting on a map how you will navigate your startup, sets where you are headed and what you are attempting to do. It helps give direction to your team. The mission explains why the company exists and what impact it is trying to make in the industry or society. After being clear on a mission, the next step is developing a strategic plan. This plan explains how to work toward the mission in consideration of the state of the market, competition, and available resources.

A strategic plan is not a mere statement of high-level goals but also expresses how you are going to get there. A good strategic plan answers how you are going to achieve your mission by covering questions such as: What are the main objectives, what is the resource needed, how do you plan on tracking your progress, and most importantly, it allows you room for flexibility to adapt to market changes.

Zomato is a perfect example. What started as a mission, in 2008, to make dining easier for users by publishing restaurant menus and reviews online, grew over time into an ambitious strategic mission: to change the way people experience food around the world. Their strategy built around this shift redefinition of their mission: from restaurant discovery to now adding food delivery, dining reservation, and even grocery delivery.

Zomato planned the same step by step. First, they enhanced the presence of the company in India by enhancing cities and restaurants. Then, after international expansion, they customized services according to regional needs and concentrated on building a strong tech platform. This strategic planning allowed them to diversify offerings, stay competitive, and adapt to the market while letting them become a household name in the food-tech industry.

This is a classic example of how Zomato's clearly defined mission and adaptable strategy contributed to its growth from a niche startup to a global leader, showcasing the power of effective strategic planning.

Customer Acquisition Channels and Techniques

Acquiring and retaining customers is very vital to the growth and sustainability of any startup. It all depends on finding appropriate channels to reach your target audience and then applying effective techniques so that they engage longer with you. Customer acquisition channels can be divided into two categories, namely online and offline strategies, and in this regard, both are equal in terms of building a loyal customer base.

Acquiring New Customers:
Many startups use a combination of digital marketing, for example, SEO, social media marketing, and content marketing, to attract potential customers. Paid advertising, such as Google Ads and Facebook Ads, allows a company to reach an audience that is much larger based on demographics and interests. Referral

programs also have a huge role in acquiring customers in that they turn the existing customer into an advocate who brings in new business to the company. Further, email marketing and collaborating with influencers or other brands can create leads while pushing conversion.

Keeping Customers Engaged:
For each customer obtained, it is more likely that you will retain them. Two tactics to create loyalty are personalization and excellent customer service. Periodically engaging a customer through personalized e-mails, loyalty offers, or special deals makes customers feel included. Gathering and acting on feedback shows customers that your business values them, hence increasing their attachment to your brand.

Techniques for Retention:
This would mean that to encourage repeat customers, value creation and seamless experience have to be primary. Features such as subscription models or continuous product and service updates ensure that a customer remains engaged. Creating a community through social media groups or forums could be a wonderful thing for long-term relationships because it gives consumers space to interact and share their experiences about your brand.

Amazon is a great example of acquisition and retention at its finest. In the beginning, the company, through aggressive pricing combined with free shipping promotions, attracted new customers with the enormous selection available. In the mix was digital advertising, affiliate programs, and email marketing to get potential buyers‘ eyes on merchandise.

Amazon Prime membership has utterly transformed the way customers maintain retention. Providing a long list of advantages, such as fast delivery, exclusive video streams, and special discounts to its users, Prime continuously attracts repeat customers. That is to say, this kind of subscription model drives repeat business and frequent repurchases with the goal of achieving loyalty and a stronger interaction with the platform in the long term.

This way Amazon is the leading e-commerce company worldwide, not only acquiring but also retaining clients by constant innovation and even giving personal recommendations according to historical behaviour.

Thus, a balanced approach in terms of acquiring channels, keeping customers engaged, and fostering loyalty can help any startup build a sustainable customer base that is profitable.

Sales Tactics: Closing Deals and Building Relationships

Sales are often compared to giving someone a toffee experience that is sweet, memorable, and makes you want some more. According to startups, a thoughtful sales strategy could be the next unlocking button to success. Whether it is about closing the deal or building a long-lasting relationship, perfecting the art of sales significantly affects the growth and sustainability of any business.

The first vital component of sales is closing deals. This extends much more than just making one transaction - it demands understanding the needs of the customer, toward which you will need to resonate with a solution. That's where you know that the art of persuasion is not speaking but listening. You need to figure this out through the right questions about what the customer needs and, therefore, position your product as the best solution. This includes a sense of urgency, such as with limited-time offers or discounts.

But selling does not end with the closing of a deal. The forging of long-term customer relationships is what differentiates short-term wins from lasting success. Customer retention is almost as vital for any startup, and a successful sales strategy emphasizes value delivery post-sale. On-time after-sales service, collecting feedback, and responses for whatever issues they may have will result in trust being formed with customers, with them eventually becoming brand advocates.

On the other hand, a close relationship with your customers would boost word-of-mouth marketing for the business and satisfied customers acting as your ambassadors to advise the world about your business. Natural growth is way more potent than any campaign.

For example, HubSpot, an inbound marketing software company changed the face of sales. Instead of pushing down people's throats with aggressive selling tactics, HubSpot set out to educate their future customers with free resources tools, and personal support. Their selling was not about closing deals but how to understand every client's needs to build relationships that last long. Therefore, most of their customers stayed loyal and were also promoters of the product, and that was how HubSpot continued to have a massive growth rate.

Sales mean more than just getting a customer to buy a product. It has the element of leaving behind a positive experience for the customer who would want to linger there and get back again. It's the successful sales strategy that will combine closure capabilities with a focus on building relationships with the customers, making them valued, satisfied, and connected to the brand. Mastering both will help you design a sales process that fuels long-term success for your startup.

Case Study: How BoAt Navigated the Market Waters to Become India's Leading Audio Brand

Founded in 2016 by Aman Gupta and Sameer Mehta, BoAt took off from the ground in business with a specific mission in mind: to provide classy, premium audio devices, resonating with Indian consumer tastes and preferences. Staying well ahead of traditional global leaders in the field, the brand managed to create for itself a particular brand image, along with innovative sales and marketing channels that supported its journey into becoming the number one audio brand in India.

Crafting a Unique Brand Identity

BoAt positioned itself as fashionable, affordable, and Indian, understanding the audience's preferences. Unlike most other competitors, BoAt targeted combining high-quality audio with stylish, fashion-forward designs in its products, where these products looked as good as they sounded. BoAt's marketing spoke to the "lifestyle" appeal of its products as must-have accessories for young, tech-savvy Indians.

Indian celebrities and sportspersons also promoted their brand by supporting it. The vibrancy of the images and the young tone associated with social media platforms perfectly align BoAt with millennial and Gen Z consumer demographics. The brand identity, "Plugging into Nirvana," has helped BoAt connect well with Indian consumers and become a first stop for stylish yet affordable audio products.

Strategy: Setting Strategic Missions and Plan

When they started BoAt, the clear-cut goal was to make great audio products available that were representative of Indians' styles and preferences. They went into detail on the new strategies needed to introduce various new categories of products in a broad distribution channel with more channels online and offline to appeal to customer requirements.

BoAt's strong emphasis on e-commerce players like Amazon and Flipkart worked in their favour, as they were able to ride the fast-growing trend in online shopping in India across the younger demographics. Partnering with online retailers increased their access to a wider segment of consumers, and responding quickly to the demands made by the customers was further facilitated. BoAt strategically augmented its offerings by including headsets, earphones, speakers, and smartwatches to keep pace with market demand.

Customer Acquisition Channels and Techniques

BoAt used multi-channel acquisition of customers via social media engagement, influencers, and e-commerce integrations. BoAt mostly relied on Instagram, YouTube, and Facebook to access their targeted young audience base by crafting engaging content through product releases.

The brand further collaborated with several popular Indian celebrities and social media influencers, thus improving its credibility and appeal. BoAt created an idea of scarcity and a deadline by providing limited time-period discounts through online channels and flash sales. They had constant interaction through social media that helped in building the most loyal community of "BoAtheads," which contributed to some solid word-of-mouth marketing.

Sales Tactics: Closing Deals and Building Relationships

BoAt was able to convert potential customers into loyal users by talking about customer service and after-sales support. They focused more on direct engagement with the customers through feedback and assisting them directly on social media channels, creating a stronger bond between the brand and its users.

The company also utilized the insights derived from data to innovate products according to the consumer's demand. BoAt launched new colours and designs to keep their lineup fresh and relevant. Maintaining quality while keeping products affordable helped BoAt build a loyal customer base, who became repeat buyers and brand advocates.

Key Takeaways

- Strong brand identity: BoAt's focus on style, affordability, and home-ground appeal helped it convey an Indian connection.
- Focused growth strategy: E-commerce and collaboration with leaders in the market like Amazon, and Flipkart, among others, aligned perfectly well with India's emerging need for online shopping.
- Innovative acquisition: From a combination of influencer marketing, social media interaction, and strategic offers and promotions that made BoAt accessible and affordable to many, created a strong and young, loyal customer base.
- Customer-Centric Sales Strategy: BoAt garnered consumer trust through after-sales support and continuous innovation-based consumer feedback.

CHAPTER SIX

STEERING THROUGH CHALLENGES: PROBLEM-SOLVING IN STARTUPS

When entering the waters of a startup, you would not know how and where the future is bound to take you- with twists, tides, and moments that are not so clear. The trials will come, but more importantly, they become proving grounds for innovation, resilience, and growth. Entrepreneurship calls for the ability to slice through knotty problems with needle-sharp analysis, logical thinking, and flexibility in constantly changing conditions. Every challenge only reveals but is not an obstacle at all, a chance to refine strategy and discover new possibilities, building a stronger basis for the future.

This chapter tackles many of the most common and serious problems that startups face and provides practical advice on overcoming them. It will be key in guiding entrepreneurs on what point to pivot, how to keep their eyes on their financial health, and how to maintain leadership in dynamic markets. It is a set of tools and insights meant to help arm entrepreneurs with the strategy of making informed decisions in the face of adversity. The methods discussed are not theoretical; they are derived from real startups that weathered such storms and emerged stronger because of them.

Success in the startup world is not about avoiding problems but learning how to navigate them. Startups live on resilience, adaptability, and calculated risk while not minding the pressure of other external factors. When entrepreneurs are able to see challenges as innovation avenues and a means of growth, they can turn setbacks into stepping stones for success. This chapter teaches one to master the art of problem-solving, from managing minimal cash flow to adapting to changes in the market, and then sail through the turbulent waters toward implementing a path toward sustainable growth.

Common Startup Challenges and How to Overcome Them

The journey of a startup is exciting, but not without a few challenges that hone even the most consistent entrepreneurs. It includes financial constraints and operational inefficiencies, culture, and market-specific hurdles, among others. Startups have to survive and flourish all these and more. The following section covers the most prevalent challenges that startups around the world and particularly in India face. Further on, this chapter identifies actionable solutions that help overcome these challenges.

Global Challenges and Their Solutions:

1. Finding Product-Market Fit
Challenge: Many startups fail to successfully build a product because they enter the market without understanding it or its target audience.
Solution:

- Validate your product idea through proper market research and customer interviews.
- Start with a Minimum Viable Product. That means testing the demand for your product among a smaller audience before scaling.
- Iterate using feedback to ensure your solution solves real problems.

Jugaad: "Don't build a product you want—build what your customer needs." Start with a product that solves one specific pain point brilliantly-even if it's a small audience let that core solution guide your growth

2. Securing Funding
Challenge: Raising capital is one of the biggest hurdles for startups, especially for first-time founders.
Solution:

- As a beginning move, bootstrap through the initial rounds. Then, establish traction and scale up before raising external funding.
- Craft an awesome pitch on your business model, market potential, and scalability.

Jugaad: "Treat every rupee like your last." Focus on building proofs of concept through actual results. Demonstrate early success stories or revenue models to build investor confidence.

3. Building a Great Team
Challenge: Finding skilled and motivated individuals who can project your vision is challenging; even more so when resources are limited.
Solution:

- Hire for attitude and adaptability as much as for skills.
- Build a strong culture that inspires loyalty and commitment.

Jugaad: "Sell the dream, not the job." Make the team member feel like a co-creator of the vision, offering him or her a share in the journey's rewards, whether equity or recognition.

4. Managing Cash Flow

Challenge: Even profitable start-ups can suffer from cash flow problems, especially when delayed payments or unexpected expenses occur.

Solution:

- It's advisable to check cash flow using financial tools and maintain detailed budgets.
- Negotiate better pay terms with vendors and seek faster collections from clients.

Jugaad: "Make every rupee work twice as hard." Reinvest your profits smartly and consider swapping services or skills to save cash in marketing or operations.

5. Adapting to Market Changes

Challenge: The market dynamics can change overnight due to shifting customer preferences or economic and technological advances.

Solution:

- Stay ahead of the curve and be willing to tweak when it becomes necessary.
- Innovation 24/7 to be ahead of the curve.

Jugaad: "Ride the wave, don't fight it." Tackle every new development in life as a challenge and ride the wave of change as an opportunity to reach new markets, expand your offerings, or become among the first to tackle a nascent trend.

Challenges Specific to Indian Startups and Their Solutions:

1. Navigating India's Diverse Market
Challenge: Indian markets are diversified in terms of languages, culture, and expenditure behaviour, making it difficult to target a single audience.
Solution:

- Target your offerings, from language to pricing strategy to the specific region.
- Conduct regional research to localize your offerings based on regions.

Jugaad: "Think regional, act national." Start small in one city or region, get the model right, and then scale across India, making appropriate adjustments for diversity.

2. Price Sensitivity and Negotiation Culture
Challenge: Indian customers are quite sensitive to price and typically negotiate extensively.
Solution:

- Offer value for money, keeping prices transparent.
- Use discounts, loyalty programs, or flexible pricing models to entice and keep customers in business.

Jugaad: "Win hearts, not just wallets." Keep your customers by over-delivering value such as surprise freebies, great service, or personalized offers.

3. Infrastructure Challenges
Challenge: Poor infrastructure, logistics, and internet connectivity might negatively impact operations, especially in Tier-2 and Tier-3 cities.
Solution:

- Set up partnerships with reliable logistics providers and employ effective supply chain solutions.
- Develop mobile applications that are fluent even at low bandwidths.

Jugaad: "Solve for the last mile first." Tackle the smallest, most proximal logistics or connectivity issues in your market; these often are the most important pain points.

4. Navigating Bureaucracy and Compliance
Challenge: Indian startups face delays and challenges in bureaucratic processes and complex regulatory requirements.
Solution:

- Leverage government initiatives such as Startup India for faster approvals and tax benefits.
- Work with regulatory advisors who can ensure compliance.

Jugaad: "Find allies, not hurdles." Build relationships with officials, advisors, and mentors who can guide you through India's confusing regulatory landscape much more quickly.

5. Payment Delays and Cash Flow Issues
Challenge: Payment delays from clients or customers are common, leading to cash flow issues.
Solution:

- Introduce strict payment terms and remind using invoicing tools.
- Build long-term relationships with clients to gain trust and timely payments.

Jugaad: "Plan for delays, not miracles." Always make provisions for delayed payments in financial planning and always ensure diversified streams of income to avoid dependence on a single client.

Challenges are an integral part of the journey of a startup, but they are also a proving ground for the real innovative and growth story. Every challenge, whether raising funds or assembling the right team that can navigate the diversities of India, is an opportunity to learn and adapt and come back stronger. Startups do not thrive by avoiding challenges but by facing them with grit and resourcefulness. With mind and creative solutions-even the toughest hurdles can become stepping stones into a sea of success for entrepreneurs, and shape their ideas into impactful ventures.

Indian startups come with different types of stakes and often with a higher degree of risk. Be it dealing with price-sensitive consumers or infrastructural shortcomings, innovative solutions such as jugaads transform potentially terrifying problems into a real goal. This is the kind of challenge that tests not only the strength of business models but also the will of its founders. These are the ones who set out to pave the way for a prospering entrepreneurial ecosystem. The true essence of a startup's success and long-term impact comes from its ability to overcome adversities with creativity and persistence.

Pivoting: When and How to Change Direction

This probably stands to be the most strategic and decisive decision a startup will ever make. It may simply mean shifting the course of a business to align much better with market needs, or for that matter, customer needs, or perhaps due to unforeseen challenges. It doesn't necessarily mean abandoning the vision in the first place but to learn from your mistakes and build on those insights to become something more impactful. In today's startup world, with all this flexibility and adaptability around, a pivot may mean the difference between failure and phenomenal success.

When Is It Important to Pivot?

The best pivot occurs when the pivot moment happens. Entrepreneurs should be able to analyse their business model, product, and market for hints that something must change:

- Product-Market Fit is not happening: Your product is not solving an important problem, or no customer cares enough about it.
- Persistent Negative Feedback: Customer complaints point out more and more issues that cannot be solved within the current framework.
- Industry Trend Shifts: Shift in the industry trend, new competitors, or changes in the economy that decrease the relevance of the way it is currently being done.
- Economics that are Unsustainable: That means costs are greater than revenues and cannot get closer with optimization.
- Emerging Opportunities: Sometimes a pivot is not about avoiding failure but instead taking advantage of something better and more profitable.

How to Pivot Effectively:

A pivot should be a calculated move, not a knee-jerk reaction. Here's how to do it successfully:

- Retain Your Core Mission: The pivot should align with your startup's fundamental vision and values. It's about improving your approach, not changing your identity.
- Leverage Existing Resources: Use your existing assets—customer base, technology, or expertise—as the foundation for your pivot.
- Listen to Stakeholders: Involve your team, investors, and customers in the process. Transparency builds trust and ensures alignment.
- Test Before Scaling: Validate the new direction by starting small. This minimizes risk and provides valuable feedback before full-scale implementation.
- Communicate Clearly: Whether it's your team or your customers, explain why the pivot is happening and how it benefits them.

One of the most iconic examples of a successful pivot is Zomato. First launched in 2008 as Foodiebay, it was a restaurant menu listing platform that achieved traction, eventually hitting a wall. The two founders realized that convenience was going to become a huge factor for customers in the rapidly expanding urban landscape. Seizing this opportunity, they pivoted into food delivery services, utilizing the restaurant database and user base they had already built.

The bold move transformed Zomato's identity into one of India's most successful startups. Today, the brand name Zomato is a household name for food delivery and is a multi-faceted, global, food-tech company. Their pivot marked the importance of making an adaptation in line with market demands yet staying firm to the core mission of elevating customer convenience.

Pivoting is not the end when things are not going right-it is a plan to remain current and relevant in a continuously shifting market. Knowing when and how to pivot allows entrepreneurs to turn unambiguously abhorrent into fantastic opportunities for stronger and sustainable businesses. Staying committed to the mission and embracing change is key in helping startups navigate the toughest challenges to become leaders in their industries.

Managing Cash Flow and Financial Health

Cash flow is the inflow and outflow of money in any business: the lifeline of any startup. It ensures that a company can meet operational expenses, seize growth opportunities, and weather unexpected challenges. Even the most profitable startups can fail if cash flow is not properly managed. Thus, founders need to optimize inflows versus outflows. Cash flow management effectively starts by tracking and periodically forecasting the finances to determine where and when the shortfall will occur. A startup may negotiate longer payment terms with the vendor while offering discounts to get payments faster from the clients. Controlling unnecessary expenses and saving cash for emergencies brings financial stability and other techniques such as issuing invoices early and leasing instead of buying will conserve liquidity.

Liquidity acts as a buffer for the short-term survival of any company, but sustaining good financial health will determine the long-term performance of any company. Financial health mirrors the ability of a business to generate profit, manage debt, and maintain stability in uncertainties. Generating diversified sources of revenue through offering complementary products or services reduces reliance on one revenue stream and stabilizes cash inflow. The wise investment in growth opportunities and prudent reinvestment in profit margins and expenses, including marketing or technology, ensure that a business remains competitive and scalable. Every startup has to set long-term financial visions and align resources for what the firm needs for future goals.

An excellent cash flow and financial health management is the case of Paytm-one of India's leading fintech companies. It expanded its offerings after starting with mobile recharge that included e-wallets, UPI payments, and financial services strategically. It ensures an almost never-ending inflow into the company, which allows it to reinvest in building a robust digital ecosystem. Managing finances with appropriate foresight helped Paytm grow continuously as well as innovate simultaneously. If managing cash flow and fostering financial fitness are not survival strategies but the base from which a resilient and thriving business rises to chase and achieve any goal, then mastering these principles will allow startups to transform financial challenges into growth opportunities and long-term success.

Dealing with Competition and Market Changes

Competition and market changes are inevitable in this dynamic space of start-ups. They are not a challenge alone but opportunities for innovation, differentiation, and excellence. For this, start-ups need to craft and bring a strategy that will help them stand out, adapt, and respond in keeping with the ever-changing demands of the market. What sets it apart is first to understand what the competitors are about knowing their strengths and weaknesses but above all being able to differentiate what makes an offering unique. The differentiation lies in the superiority of quality or innovative features or unmatched customer experience. Take the case of BoAt, an Indian audio brand, in a crowded market, that carved a niche in stylish, affordable products catered to the needs of Indian millennials, making even competition an advantage.

To maintain your lead, develop a relationship with customers through personalized experiences, loyalty programs, and other exceptional services. Loyal customers give you guaranteed revenue besides being the biggest advocates of your brand. Continuous innovation also becomes important; investment in the research and development arm will help you go beyond what the customer expects and ahead of competitors. Agility is another cornerstone of success; regularly check and monitor competitors and market trends, and be ready to pivot or change strategies. A strong brand identity plays a very important role and helps consumers connect to your values, and you are chosen over others.

Following market trends requires an active attitude. Pay attention to the latest trends, consumers, and technology. For example, during the COVID-19 era, Zomato timely offered groceries through delivery because consumers also began ordering, and during that time, delivering groceries was a crucial source of income; similarly, maintaining various streams of revenue would be critical to stability in areas where fluctuations are impossible to prevent. Listening to customer feedback is equally important-understanding their evolving needs allows you to align your offerings with market demands well.

Building long-term success is achieved through the use of technological capabilities and through necessary collaborative partnerships that invest in a qualified, motivated team able to work through the changing scenarios. The competition and changes within the market are not obstacles, but growth drivers. Therefore, using such challenges with innovation, agility, and customer orientation, startups can transform these barriers into opportunities and be the market leaders in these dynamic business situations.

CHAPTER SEVEN

MAPPING GROWTH: SCALING YOUR STARTUP

It is the most exciting yet challenging time for an entrepreneur taking his business from survival to really blossoming, taking it from a small niche audience to a much larger market. Scaling is not just growth but expansion in a smart and sustainable way. This would be the optimization of processes, embracing technology, and preparation for increased demand without losing quality or effectiveness in serving their customers. Scaling ensures that a foundation is in place-one that can support growth while maintaining the essence and principles that make a startup singular.

This chapter deals with the art and science of scaling, offering actionable strategies for entrepreneurs on how to navigate what is very often one of the most critical phases. It balances between ambition and pragmatism-it knows when to take risks and when to consolidate strengths. It builds a scalable business model that grows without having costs increase disproportionately, increases operations, and invests in the right team and infrastructure to support that growth. It has to be predictable as much as nimble-be it venturing into new markets, automation, or new streams of revenue. And every decision taken today must work toward your long-term vision while solving the next day's problem.

In today's competitive environment, scaling also means staying agile and being prepared for change. Market dynamics shift quickly, and startups must be ready to refine strategies or pivot to maintain relevance. This chapter provides the insights and tools needed to achieve that balance. Through proven frameworks and real-world examples, you'll learn how to scale your startup in a way that ensures sustainable success. Scaling is not just growing in size but growing in excellence in the process, so preparing your business for long-term impact and leadership in its industry.

Strategies for Scaling Operations

Scaling operations is one of the most important milestones toward changing a small venture startup into a thriving company. In other words, it means not just an increase in the number of processes but the optimization of processes that can accommodate increased demand without affecting efficiency, quality, and customer satisfaction. Thus, intelligent scaling enables companies to be able to achieve sustainable growth to meet market demand for improved profitability as well. Management streamlines operations, prevents delays, consistently delivers excellent value, and exceeds the expectations of customers. Efficient scaling also optimizes costs through minimal waste and productivity improvement and therefore creates an advantage in the market. In addition, a scalable operational framework opens up resources. Businesses are then able to invest the freed resources into innovation and continually improve what they offer. Scaling is not a choice but the lifeblood of any successful, sustainable growth that any entrepreneur hopes to create in a truly impactful company.

Strategies for Scaling Operations:

- Process optimization by automation: Automate all the processes that are time-consuming and repetitive in nature. Then, tools like CRM systems, automatic inventory management, or AI-based analytics can be effectively used for managing vast data volumes to make business processes streamlined. Example: Swiggy is a startup that uses AI-enabled logistics to optimize the route for food delivery and ensures it is faster and cheaper in terms of operations.
- Technology Offerings: Scaling actually demands adopting technology, and its efficiency can be yielded through cloud computing, digital payment systems, and advanced data analytics. For example, Flipkart created a robust e-commerce platform with having scalable technical infrastructure which allowed them to handle millions of users and transactions in seamless manners.
- Focus on core competencies: Identify what your company does best and double down on it. Outsource non-core functions such as payroll, customer support, or logistics to specialized this way you would allocate more resources toward activities that directly drive growth.
- Create an Agile Workforce: Upscaling usually means serving a variable demand flow. Hire a combination of full-timers, freelancers, and contractors to be flexible. Training programs to improve the team's proficiency in handling growing pains.
- Scalable Processes from Day One: Engineering workflows that can take on increased demand from the start matters. Whether it's inventory management, customer service, or delivery systems, make sure there are scalable elements integrated right from the start so there is no blocking elsewhere.

- Strengthen Supply Chain and Logistics: As you scale, your supply chain should scale too. Work with dependable suppliers, utilize real-time tracking devices, and diversify supplier lists for the smooth flow of goods and services.
- Review KPIs: Review how well your scaling has been serving you by keeping tabs on delivery times, customer satisfaction, and cost efficiency. Periodic review will keep you in tune and adjust operations to different situations.

Building a Scalable Business Model

A scalable business model is the basic structure of sustainable and exponential growth for any startup. It allows for an increase in operations and revenue streams without a proportional rise in costs, so profitability and efficiency are retained as the company grows. A well-designed scalable model is one which, with growing customer demand, will change the shape of the business to scale and not create additional strain on resources while maintaining quality or disrupting customer experience. It is not about doing more; it is building systems, processes, and strategies that work at any scale.

A scalable business model starts by understanding what are the core strengths and resources that your startup can deploy in ways to amplify it. It will highly benefit your business as automation reduces manual efforts and bottlenecks for repeats of processes. It would drive efficiency, cost minimization, and seamlessness in growth as the company grows along with technology. For instance, CRM tools offer ready and streamlined approaches to accessing and retaining customers. The analytical tools enable insights and data analysis for the purposes of decision-making.

Scalability also involves developing products or services that can be sold to a large audience without requiring much customization or manual intervention. Think of models easy to replicate and scale, such as subscription-based services or digital platforms. Adaptability is equally important for startups: models have to be flexible enough to change with shifts in markets and technologies.

It is not about growing revenue at all but doing it in an efficient and sustainable way. That way, the business would stay agile and competitive, seize new opportunities, master unforeseen challenges, and preserve its crux and vision.

Flipkart is the epitome of a scalable business model. The leading Indian e-commerce entity was actually launched as an online bookstore in 2007 with the purpose of streamlining operations and designing a technology platform that could cope with growing volume and transactions.

Flipkart invested in the logistics infrastructure to scale correctly. This was a robust supply chain that would get millions of products delivered. The company also followed the marketplace model, where it added third-party sellers, increasing its offerings without holding much inventory at one go. Overheads reduced because it catered to the increasing demands of its customers. Customer data was also used for personalization purposes and to improve this engagement metric, sales worldwide increased because of it.

The company mushroomed from a small start-up to become a giant household name in Indian e-commerce by applying technology, partnerships, and data-driven decision-making. This was achieved by adapting a scalable model, where growth was rapid while simultaneously placing itself as a leader to compete with international giants like Amazon.

Any start-up that seeks sustained growth and profitability requires a scalable business model. The most effective way to acquire scale is through the optimization of process automation, implementation of available technology, and establishing systems that can increase without loss of efficiency and quality. Flipkart is the best example; scalability creates a business viable in competitive markets with this type of approach. Therefore, a scalable business model appropriate to the situation is not a strategy for entrepreneurs but the base on which vision may be translated into long-term success.

Expanding Your Team and Infrastructure

A scaling startup needs to scale the team and infrastructure to support increased demands in a growth process. Even though a lean setup is acceptable for early stages of growth, strong, skilled professionals and efficient systems are needed to manage complexity when a business scales. The expansion of your team will provide the expertise and diverse perspectives you need to take on new challenges. Upgrading your infrastructure will create the capacity to support heavier workloads in a faster, more efficient, and maintainable way. That is the growth phase: not adding more but doing so strategically and productively that fits within your long-term vision.

When you are building your team, you are hiring for fit and cultural fit, as well as technical skills. People you're hiring should bring the technical expertise required to solve the immediate challenge but share the same values and mission of the company. This will contribute to better collaboration and long-term loyalty. Core roles fill in operations, marketing, customer service, and technology as you grow, but freelancers and consultants can bridge gaps with less long-term expense commitments. Of course, you also invest in training programs to upskill your teams and make leaders responsible for their domains. You delegate authority, create trust, and ownership to grow a good team.

Any emerging startup's infrastructure should change as its team changes. Technology upgrades-also known as cloud computing, automated systems-increase the efficiency and scalability of organizations. Increasing physical spaces and optimized supply chains and scalable workflows are some of the things that allow operation to absorb augmented demands without having their quality reduced. Even startups can opt for flexible solutions like co-working space, leased equipment, and cloud storage, which may allow rapid scaling while keeping up-front costs to the barest minimum. Strategic infrastructure development will ensure that your business can expand systematically.

Consider Ola. When it expanded its ride-hailing business all over India, it was taking support to expand its team strength with the help of local market experts and training the drivers in depth for consistent seamless services. At the same time, Ola was making investments into a strong technology platform that could support millions of transactions every day. Thus, this strategy of team expansion and infrastructure development simultaneously at the same pace helped Ola to scale fast and still maintain operational excellence.

Strategic recruitment and building of teams and infrastructure are the canvases for sustainable growth. Only deliberate, thoughtful decisions by startups can allow them to meet increasing market demand, increase efficiency, and ultimately make great strides toward long-term success.

Global Expansion: Taking Your Startup International

Expansion to an international market for your startup is a major milestone, unlocking mammoth growth opportunities, diversified revenue streams, and increased brand identity. But it's not about replicating your home success on an international platform; rather, it is about getting an understanding of and adapting to unique dynamics in each of the new markets. Internationalization is very easy for Indian startups since they can make use of the global positioning of India in terms of innovation and talent. The internationalization of a startup is done after proper planning, cultural awareness, and adaptation to a variety of regulations and customer behaviours.

How to Take Your Startup International:

- Understand the New Market: Carry out thorough research about the market, understanding your customers' needs, cultural differences, and demand in a target country.
- Start Small: Focus on one or two markets that align with the idea your startup is projecting, have fewer barriers to entering a new market, and concentrate on creating a solid footing first before moving on to harder areas.
- Local Partnerships: Look for local partners or distributors. These can be very instrumental in gaining local insights and minimizing the operational challenges experienced in foreign markets while generating credibility in the market.
- Tailor Your Product or Service: Ensure that your product or service is in tune with local tastes, habits, and expectations. Chai Point, for example, being an Indian startup, can make its brand resonate well with a whole culture of tea around the world but still be Indian at its core.
- Legal and Regulatory Environment: Observe the local laws, tax regulations, and trade policies to avoid an operational setback.

Why International Expansion Is Important:

- Diversified Revenue Streams: Exploring other markets reduces the dependence on domestic revenue and yields stability in economic turbulence.

- Brand Value Enhancement: International presence enhances credibility and presents your startup as a leader in its sector.
- Access to Larger Markets: Going global opens up opportunities to tap into larger and more lucrative customer bases.

Tips for Expanding Internationally:

- Leverage Digital Channels: Use online platforms to test the waters in international markets without heavy upfront investment. Digital marketing and e-commerce platforms like Amazon Global are excellent starting points.
- Focus on Scalability: Ensure your operational model is scalable and efficient to handle international demands.
- Hire Local Talent: Building a team with local expertise ensures better customer engagement and cultural alignment.
- Use Government Initiatives: Take advantage of programs like Startup India and Make in India, which encourage Indian entities to enter the global market.
- Learn From the Competition: Identify how other similar businesses were able to expand globally and replicate this but with your own Flavors.

Radhika Aggarwal, the co-founder of ShopClues, is the epitome of how a woman-led startup can scale up its operations and expand in a competitive market. Starting as an online marketplace to offer affordable, locally sourced products to Indian consumers in 2011, ShopClues had to face stiff competition from giants like Flipkart and Amazon. However, the vision was clear with Radhika: empower small and medium-sized businesses by giving them a platform to reach a broader audience.

This also helped ShopClues be focused on unique value

propositions such as catering to the tier-2 and tier-3 cities, for a variety of budget-priced products. This strategy in turn enabled the company not only to scale rapidly in the Indian markets but also make a path for global scaling by capturing the demand in the market for affordable varied goods. Radhika is a planning strategist who aligns partnerships with technology enablement of operations, all moving toward the natural progression in global scaling.

Her journey demonstrates how a startup needs to go international by understanding both the local and global markets with a scalable business model as well as relentless adaptability. ShopClues under the helm of Radhika Aggarwal remains a strong reminder that in a competitive market, it is possible for a born-in-a-startup venture to make it big around the world.

Taking your startup internationally is a very ambitious and rewarding endeavour. It would provide Indian startups with the opportunity to showcase their innovation on the world stage while tapping into diverse markets. Conducting extensive research, adapting to local needs, and building strong local partnerships are good ways that will help knock down the challenge of international expansion. When done strategically and executed well, expansion global offers growth and sets up your startup as a global leader in its industry.

CHAPTER EIGHT

Staying on Course: Leadership and Company Culture

Leadership and company culture are the twin pillars of any successful startup: they guide it through challenges and shape its identity as it grows. Leadership is not just decision-making but inspiring teams, fostering innovation, and having a clear vision. Leaders act like navigators, ensuring that the company aligns with its mission while adapting to changes in a dynamic business environment. They facilitate, empower teams, and inculcate a culture of trust and accountability so that they become a part of the startup's journey.

Shared values, beliefs, and practices that define how people work together are just as important as company culture. This is the secret to a positive culture that communicates and sets up an environment where employees feel valued, motivated, and connected to the company's purpose-the driving factor for collaboration, creativity, loyalty, and the backbone of long-term success. When harmonized and functioning for each other, leadership and culture are the most powerful assets that a startup has resilient, innovative, cohesive-and able to thrive despite problems. This chapter discusses the potential profound role that leadership and culture can play for startups navigating toward sustainable growth and long-term impact.

Effective Leadership in a Growing Startup

Leadership is the main foundation upon which any successful start-up business can be established, mainly during the developmental stage. During this period, challenges and opportunities may emerge at lightning speed. Good leadership in an expanding startup would not only mean making the decisions but also inspiring your team, building trust and motivating people toward a set vision while remaining agile enough to respond to changing situations. The best leader inspires his team, empowers them, motivates them, and aligns them to his company's vision.

In the initial stages of any business, leaders generally tend to be responsible for strategic planning and daily operations as well as many more things. As the business grows, though, it becomes a lot different. The role of the leader changes to more strategic in nature, which means many things have to be delegated. Delegation allows the leadership to focus on scaling the operations, entering new markets, and creating partnerships. Delegation also creates ownership in a team, thereby increasing productivity and morale.

Another characteristic of leadership in a startup is clarification and clear communication. The increasing team should be well-versed on the company's vision and the way their input is channelled into the achievement of the same. Serenity can only be achieved through continuous communication alone, and the same feeling of trust is developed. The leader must be reachable and understanding to the needs of the members who would require considerable direction.

Adaptability is one of the most significant characteristics of effective leadership within an emerging startup. Market dynamics shift, customer preferences transform, and competition intensifies. An effective leader remains receptive to innovative concepts and is prepared to modify approaches. For instance, during its initial expansion phase, Ola responded to fluctuating customer needs by implementing features like ride-sharing and bike taxis, showing that forward-thinking leadership calls for the identification of leadership opportunities.

Finally, a startup leader must lead from the front. Whether it is upholding the work ethic, embracing challenges, or holding the company values, every leader's behaviour sets the tone for an organization. Leaders play an extremely crucial role in converting startups into flourishing businesses through inspiring confidence, building collaboration, and wise decision-making.

Good leadership is not perfect. It's real, flexible, and focused on the success of the team and the company. If great leadership were applied to a startup, then challenges would become opportunities, and dreams are presented with reality.

Fostering a Positive and Productive Culture

Company culture is the soul of any organization, which describes how people interact and work. The same applies to a startup; when business culture is positive and productive, it sets a tone that will determine growth, innovation, and teamwork. Companies with great cultures not only attract better talent but also keep their employees motivated, engaged, and on the same wavelength as the company. It is this intangible, invisible bond that holds the team together, creating an atmosphere for everyone to thrive in.

A clear-positive culture begins with well-defined values. Startups should define and communicate their core principles, such as transparency, respect, creativity, and customer-centricity. Such values guide behaviour and decision-making, hence working together to achieve a common goal. Many successful startups adopt an "open-door policy," encouraging open communication and collaboration between team members and the leadership. That not only cultivates trust but also builds a sense of belonging.

A productive culture enables employees to operate at full capacity. Providing the right tools and resources and having the support structure in place is therefore quite important. Flexible work policies, recognition programs, and professional opportunities can contribute positively to productivity and morale. Healthy work-life balances are also crucial for attacking burnout and ensuring long-term engagement.

Startups that celebrate diversity and inclusion create innovative and dynamic cultures. Welcoming those from different backgrounds and perspectives generates ideas and solves problems from various standpoints. For instance, the diversity and cohesion in teams at Freshworks are principles behind the company's successful globalization.

Leadership cultivates the culture. A leader, who embodies the values of the company, inspires those around him to be very much the same. Check-ins, team activities, and even giving feedback are ways to build relationships and improve continuously. Where innovation is rewarded and achievements celebrated, every employee seeks to take ownership of their work, leading to success on a personal and organizational level.

In the end, a positive and productive culture has nothing to do with just policies and perks-it is where people feel valued, supported, and motivated to contribute their best. This is precisely what culture does for startups and places them one step ahead of the competition to help them attract and retain talent, navigate challenges, and emerge in the long run as victors.

Managing Teams and Conflict Resolution

The backbone of growth and success to any startup is effective management of the team. A well-coordinated team collaborates and prospers on mutual understanding, shared vision, and seamless coordination of difference purposes toward the accomplishment of the company's goals. No matter which shape they take, startups assemble diverse groups of individuals possessing diverse skill sets and backgrounds-a recipe for creativity and innovation. This diversity, on the other hand, however brings about some misunderstandings, conflict of ideas, or even conflict if it goes unchecked. Smooth teamwork, therefore ensures that every member is on the right track; well-defined roles, communication, and a basis of trust and respect. If harmoniously working, a team would produce an environment that brings about creativity, efficiency to peak levels, and steadily grows the company.

Conflicts are inevitable in the dynamic and fast-paced environment of a startup. These may come from differences in opinions, competing priorities, or misunderstandings about each other's communications. Conflict resolution in and out is not only important but also crucial in maintaining an upbeat and collaborative culture. Unresolved conflict can fester, resulting in poor morale, lousy performance, and possibly disrupting the startup's forward momentum. Conflicting ends often point at the underlying cause of the problem. That deals with listening to all who have an interest in the matter, understanding the perspective of others, and finding room for open respectful communication regarding the issue. Work should always be directed to solving the problem, not fault-finding.

Conflicts are opportunity for growth, not barriers. Leaders are responsible for solution-oriented culture. Conflict resolution then will be effective not only in solving the problem but also in trust and collaboration, as well as the innovative skills. Then only will conflict be handled after one finds the root cause, which is done through keen listening to the involved parties. In an open area devoid of judgment, there could be free airing of their concerns by team members paving the way for solutions.

Thus, the common problem is solved through shifting the team's attention to the problem and not to the person. In case of acute problems, using neutral language for communication, and mediating may nullify the tensions and push toward a move toward resolving the situation. For instance, if two departments frustrate over the priorities they have been following, a leader can change the priority through shifting the focus on shared goals as well as a larger goal of the company. Following through on the solutions and monitoring ensures sustainability.

In startups, head-on confrontation of conflicts leads to resilient and cohesive teams where agility and collaboration are essential. Leaders who handle disputes with empathy and decisiveness not only resolve issues but inspire loyalty and a culture of mutual respect that will keep the firm on the track for growth and success.

For instance, Infosys, the most dominant IT company of India, had its fair share of disagreement between the founders in the initial stages. Instead of letting this disagreement divert their vision, the team had open and honest discussions that allowed them to agree on this matter. In doing so, it not only solved the immediate issues but also made their bond stronger by establishing a long-term precedent of collaborative decision-making, which ultimately led to the company's success.

Balancing Vision with Practicality

Balancing vision with practicality is like a ship through uncharted waters. Your vision is your destination: the "where" you wanted to go and, in contrast, the "how-to-get-there" would form your practicality in navigating. As an entrepreneur, dream big, but make sure that the dreams are not delusional but grounded in reality instead. Without balance, your start-up will either drift aimlessly or set sail toward the horizon of an unrealistic dream. The thing about longevity is that the best success usually marries the boldness of vision with the pragmatism to fulfil that vision.

While vision inspires and propels your team forward, practicality ensures that each step you take is doable and sustainable. Think of your vision as a skyscraper—ambitious and towering. But without a solid foundation, such as strong processes, proper funding, or a well-structured plan, your skyscraper will never rise. Practicality is about how to break down your grand ideas into smaller, manageable tasks, measure them, and execute them strategically. Every entrepreneur must ask themselves: What do I need to do today to get closer to where I want to be?

Scalability happens step-by-step. Startups need to identify what can be achieved in the short term while keeping their eyes fixed on the long-term goals. In that case, if your vision is built for becoming a global brand, you need to focus first on making a locally or regionally market-leading product and then grow slowly to cultivate loyalty from strong customers. Take the example of Zomato. Zomato's founders had a vision to change the way people dine worldwide, but they started by dominating the Indian market and then scaling across the world once they had optimized their core offerings. The specific actions they took-polymerizing their product, optimizing their operations, and going up incrementally-enabled them to scale sustainably and stay on track toward their larger vision.

Flexibility is another key element that bridges vision with pragmatism. The market is always evolving, and there is no guarantee that what is working today will work tomorrow. Being inflexible over your vision can inversely limit your growth. The best leaders indeed understand how to adjust strategy when appropriately needed, without losing the bigger vision. Ola, which was originally a taxi service only, realized the deep need for electric vehicles and easily innovated its offerings. By continuously refining their business model, Ola was able to stay relevant and expand both domestically and internationally.

The way you're going to balance vision with practicality would be through a combination of measurable goals, being flexible, and the ability to work toward detailed next steps that can be measured and tracked. Ask yourself, "What are some small but highly meaningful ways that I can take steps toward that larger goal? What is the underlying resource that is needed?" Align daily decisions with larger objectives, all of which bring you closer to your vision.

Ultimately, balancing vision with practicality is how big ideas are converted into concrete action. It refers to taking that golden point between dreaming too big and being down-to-earth enough in such a way that the startup's vision is inspiring but also achievable. Such entrepreneurship can help build an enduring business in which the nexus between innovation and strategy is found.

CHAPTER NINE

Weathering the Storm: Managing Risk and Failure

It is a journey that is indeterminate, uncertain at every turn, full of unexpected hurdles, and the occasional storm of challenges that can test your mettle. Risk and failure are not obstacles to be feared but are a natural part of this path; rather, they are inevitable companions on this journey. Success stories of startups are not about the ones who avoided risks but about the ones that learned the art of wisely managing them and turning failures into powerful growth lessons.

Every decision that a startup makes comes with risk. Be it the financial investment or which market strategy to pursue, risks may determine if it will be a defining factor in your company or break its trajectory. However, with careful planning, sharp foresight, and flexibility, risks can therefore be opportunities for growth. Failure is not the end of the road but a detour in life. The best entrepreneurs have had failures that gave them resilience, innovation, and persistence.

Going beyond risks and failures, this chapter also shines light on the very important yet commonly overlooked aspect of life in startups: mental health and work-life balance. Even the most motivated people get their feet held on the fire with the constant stress and pressure of a startup environment. Preserving your well-being will keep you sharp, focused, and ready for leadership through trying times.

Crises are a natural part of starting a business but do not predict the future. Be it a sudden financial downturn, operational breakdown, or reputation crisis, having a strategy in place will enable you to react quickly and accordingly. This chapter gives you the tools, strategies, and real-world insights to navigate risks, learn from failures, and handle crises with confidence. It is, therefore, the navigation of such storms that will define your startup and not the storms themselves.

Risk Management Strategies for Startups

Risk is an accompanying phenomenon in the journey of a startup because it manifests as financial uncertainties, operational challenges, market fluctuations, and regulatory hurdles, to mention but a few. It is within such risks that may either make or break the advance of a startup that comes into play effective management strategies this case, risk management. Risk management then is the proactive process of identifying, assessing, and mitigating such potential threats to such growth. For startups experiencing a high-uncertainty environment, a well-crafted risk management framework can be a safety net but significantly more-it becomes a survival and long-term success cornerstone.

Effective risk management allows for the anticipation of disruptions, streamlines operations, and builds resilience in the face of unplanned events. It allows founders to envision dangers and prepare in advance for those events while minimizing the prospect of unpleasant surprises. Moreover, a demonstrated proactive approach to risk management promotes trust among investors and other stakeholders, indicating strategic foresight and stability. Managing risks is a step-by-step process that embraces three strategic steps: identification of potential risks, such as financial or regulatory challenges; assessment of the likelihood and impact to prioritize responses; and mitigation through actionable strategies such as diversifying revenue streams, creating financial buffers, or adopting advanced cybersecurity measures.

With integrated risk management into their core strategy, startups would have the right confidence to navigate uncertainties while using potential threats to gather opportunities for growth and innovation. This approach not only ensures smoother operations but also will position the startup as a resilient and reliable player in the marketplace.

Strategies for Effective Risk Management:

- Diversify Revenue Streams: Do not put all your eggs in one basket. Relying on a single product, market, or customer base increases vulnerability to market shifts. Expanding your offerings—whether by introducing complementary products or targeting different customer demographics—helps reduce dependency and spreads risk. For instance, a tech startup offering SaaS solutions could explore consulting services or subscription-based add-ons to build a more resilient revenue base.
- Build Financial Buffers: Just as your home needs insulation and a firewall, an early-stage company needs an emergency fund or a backup credit line in case a series of unfortunate events unfolds unexpectedly. Start with a consistent percent of profits going to a month-by-month contingency fund – ensure your business has the liquidity to continue surviving lean periods or sudden

upsets.

- Risk Monitoring Technology: Technology can be an absolute game-changer for the management of risks. Engage tools such as a risk management software or analytics driven by AI to check on potential threats in real time. You can monitor your industry trends using Google Alerts or keep track of cash flows and expenses with financial tools QuickBooks or Xero, amongst many others. These technologies ensure that you are able to make decisions based on real-time data and change pace with challenges.
- Implement Clear and Strong Contracts: Shield your business relationships through the use of strong contracts. Clearly define roles and responsibilities, and contingency measures to be undertaken in agreements by partners, vendors, and employees. Include clauses on risks, such as delays or disputes, in order to ensure smooth operation even when challenges are presented. Legal foresight saves your business from unnecessary setbacks.
- Stay updated and flexible: The business environment is changing. It is always a good idea to monitor the latest trends, competitors' activities, and regulatory updates. You could subscribe to newsletters related to your industry, attend events or even use analytics tools to track changes before they affect your startup. This gives you time to adjust your strategies and grab opportunities faster than your competitors do.

Essential Tips for Mastering Risk Management in Startups:

- Regular Health Checks: Think of your startup as a living organism—routine check-ups are a must. Regularly review finances, operations, and your market position to spot risks early. This proactive approach will ensure that minor problems do not snowball into full-blown crises.

- Empower Your Team to Spot Risks: Risk management cannot be a one-person show. There are likely people on the ground who can look out for operational bottlenecks or customer pain points. Get them engaged in risk identification and risk brainstorming to inculcate shared responsibility.
- Simulate Crisis Scenarios: Only as good as its execution, a risk plan is best put to the test through simulated scenarios in the form of a major supplier delay or market shift. These drills typically reveal gaps but also prepare your team to respond well under pressure.
- Adopt a Flexible Framework: Rigidity is the enemy of risk management. Embrace agile practices that allow your startup to pivot quickly in response to unexpected challenges. Whether it's tweaking a product launch plan or reallocating resources, adaptability ensures minimal disruption.

When Flipkart started its journey in 2007, it took huge risks in the very nascent Indian e-commerce market. Internet penetration was low, and consumer confidence in online purchases and logistics issues were significant problems. However, Flipkart tackled these risks through proactive strategies in challenges-turned-opportunities.

To address the risk of consumer trust, Flipkart pioneered the "Cash on Delivery" model, which was a game-changer for e-commerce in India. The innovation mediated the risk of customers holding back their prepayment for online purchases. From the logistics standpoints, the company has developed an entirely owned supply chain network that delivers goods in a timely and reliable manner, thereby minimizing inter-dependency on third-party providers.

Flipkart managed financial risk by diversifying its revenue streams over time. The firm expanded in time from selling books to electronics, clothing, and groceries, reducing dependence on any one single product category. Flipkart also secured several rounds of funding from global investors to ensure financial stability and fuel its rapid growth.

From the identification of market-specific risks and developing solutions customised to each risk, Flipkart both overcame initial roadblocks and charted its rise as a leader in Indian e-commerce. This story informs the importance of proactive risk management in building a successful and sustainable startup.

Risk management is not about the absence of risks but the presence of preparation. By identifying, assessing, and proactively mitigating risks, startups can build resilience in a world of unpredictability. Practical strategies include diversification of revenue, embracing technology, and information sharing to allow startups to change threats into opportunities. The right approach to risk management becomes a competitive advantage, which allows startups to grow with confidence while still ready for the challenges ahead.

Learning from Failure: Turning Setbacks into Success

Failure is the end, but sometimes the end is only an adventure in a world called startups. To entrepreneurs, setbacks are not failures but rather opportunities to learn, grow, and innovate. Every mistake is being a lesson that often cannot be learned by the taste of success. In other words, failure would expose gaps in the planning phase, highlight weaknesses in execution, or even prove more deeply that there was a misunderstanding of the market. Such difficult lessons learned allow startups to recalibrate their approach, improve their strategies, and avoid repeating the same mistakes. Every failure carries in its womb some seeds of improvement, and in very many cases, the foundation for future breakthroughs.

The journey of a startup is rarely smooth; it's a path of unfamiliar twists and turns. Embracing failure as a natural part of the process is crucial for every entrepreneur. When things don't go according to plan, analyse the situation objectively. Emotions will always be natural but should never cloud judgment. Instead, take a step back to reflect on what went wrong. Was it a product-market mismatch? Bad execution? Or a lack of thorough market research? The identification of the underlying factors is the first step toward making informed, smarter decisions.

Small business owners are resilient and adaptable. An opportunity to pivot, innovate, or go a different way is just as much the result of failure as facing challenges with newfound clarity. In fact, the most remarkable success stories in the startup world originate from a history of failure-the proof that temporary setbacks are part of a bigger scheme. Entrepreneurs who develop this mindset stay focused on their ideas and remain prepared to confront future challenges with unwavering confidence. In the world of startups, failure is not a dead-end but a stepping stone into a more well-informed and driven trip to success.

Tips for Turning Setbacks into Success:

- Adopt a growth mindset: Relate failure to a stepping stone instead of a dead end. Every failure is an opportunity to learn, innovate, and grow. Don't focus on what went wrong, but rather on what you can take away from that experience and how you can do better next time.
- Dive Deep into Analysis: Do not scratch the surface when discussing a failure. Have a proper post-mortem to know the core reasons—whether it is a product-market mismatch, operational inefficiency, or misunderstanding customers. Knowing the "why" helps make informed changes.

- Reframe and Refocus Your Goals: Failure often highlights areas that need attention. Use these insights to refine your goals and strategies. Whether it's tweaking your product, entering a new market, or rethinking your customer approach, realignment after failure often sets the stage for greater success.
- Pivot with a Purpose: When failure signals that things need to shift, pivot. Pivot directionally-whether to target a new audience, rebrand, or alter your product offerings. The very resilient startups are those that could pivot quickly and decisively.
- Build Resilience Through Optimism: Resilience isn't just about enduring failure—it's about bouncing back stronger. Remind yourself to stay positive, keep your eyes on the bigger picture, and that everyone who's a successful entrepreneur has faced setbacks along the way. Challenges can be motivation to push harder.
- Seek Constructive Feedback: Do not stumble through failure alone. Talk to mentors, peers, or even customers, to get candid feedback. Novice eyes can find the blind spots and even provide new solutions.
- Document and Share Your Learnings: Recording what went wrong and how you rectified it becomes a playbook for future challenges. Sharing these lessons with the team and peers also encourages openness and collective progress.

The country's largest online lingerie retailer: had the bold dream to change the way women shopped for innerwear in a country where it remained virtually an unmentionable subject. Initial setbacks lay before it, as customers will often not purchase intimate apparel online, fearing loss of modesty and a lack of 'hands-on' experience with the product. Moreover, Zivame faced the additional challenge of educating consumers about fit and comfort in their purchases.

Instead of giving up, Zivame took these failures as a chance to refine their business approach. They put aggressive privacy policies in place along with detailed size guides and virtual fitting rooms, using technology to replicate the in-store experience online. Further on, they spent money on campaigns and workshops for customer education. It broke taboos, urging women to concentrate on comfort.

These strategies not only helped address their early setbacks but also carved a unique position in the market for Zivame. Today, Zivame is a household name in India, proving how learning from failure and addressing challenges specific to a market can turn obstacles into huge growth opportunities.

Failure is not a dead end; it is a valuable teacher. Each setback is an opportunity to innovate and adapt for an entrepreneur. By being resilient and learned, even the seemingly toughest challenges for startups can form the foundations of future success.

Maintaining Mental Health and Work-Life Balance

Entrepreneurship is exciting, but it is also incredibly demanding, rife with high stakes, long hours, and relentless pressure. While the impulse to succeed can often propel entrepreneurs into burning the midnight oil frenzies, neglecting their mental health and work-life balance can contribute to burnout and negative impacts on productivity and decision-making abilities. For entrepreneurs, mental wellness and maintaining a work-life balance are not just personal responsibilities but formational aspects of building a sustainable and successful business.

Good mental health gives an entrepreneur a clear mind, and stress is managed in a manner that does not impact the making of sound decisions. Creativity and good relationships with the team are fuelled, it brings about a good outlook even in tough scenarios. Work-life balance usually helps entrepreneurs balance professional commitments with personal lives. This can prevent burnout and ensure they have the capacity to recharge, resulting in sustained motivation and focus.

Entrepreneurs need to understand that taking care of one's mental well-being is not a symptom of weakness but a critical investment in the success of the businessman. Taking breaks or setting boundaries through simple activities can really bring great improvement in the overall life of the person. Prioritizing health doesn't detract from ambition; it strengthens it. Successful entrepreneurs like Ratan Tata have often explained that maintaining an equilibrium while valuing one's well-being, right along with professional achievements, helps translate into successful entrepreneurship.

Companies also have a responsibility to promote a mentally healthy culture. Entrepreneurs should realize that any successful business bases itself on a healthy and motivated team. A healthy and positive work environment, regular breaks, flexible working hours, and holidays can contribute much toward building morale and productivity. A culture that encourages mental health improves team dynamics, strengthens the employee's loyalty, and reduces attrition rates.

For both startups and entrepreneurs, building sustainable success is impossible without valuing mental health and work-life balance. They integrate these principles into their daily lives as well as into the cultures of their organizations, creating healthier, happier environments while also positioning themselves and their teams for long-term success. Keeping the work-life balance is not just about taking care of the self-it is ensuring that the vision thrives through the people and resources driving it forward.

Preparing for and Handling Crisis Situations

Crises are an inevitable part of running a startup. Financial setbacks, operational failures, market disruptions, and reputational risks are typical examples, but this is not all. Crises can take so many forms that one often hears warning that they may arise unexpectedly. They test resilience, adaptability, and leadership within the core teams and founders. In this regard, how a startup prepares for and handles such crises often defines its long-term success or failure. Strategically approached and proactively managed, otherwise demolishing hurdles can become great opportunities for growth, innovation, and focus.

The space a startup operates within is one of constant uncertainty with limited availability of resources, intense competition, and high risks. A poorly managed crisis can quickly derail progress, damage reputation, and ultimately threaten the very survival of a company. For example, a sudden issue in cash flow could affect the operations, or a negative customer review could go viral negative reception from public opinion. However, a well-prepared startup with a reliable crisis management plan can confront such turbulence confidently and keep its stability intact.

Effective crisis management is not just about managing damage; it is protecting the greatest resources your company owns, including your people, finances, and reputation, ensuring that stakeholder trust remains intact. Successful startups often emerge from their crises stronger, wiser and sharpened in focus. The four pillars of turning difficult into stepping stones for future success are preparation, swift action, clear communication, and being solution-oriented. In the world of startups, every problem has seeds of opportunity. How you handle the storm is what determines whether you sink or soar.

Common Crisis Situations in Startups:

- Financial Crises: Cash flow shortage, loss of funding, and unexpected expenses directly pose operational challenges.
- Operational Failures: Disruptions in the supply chain, technical faults, or production delays can affect service delivery.
- Market Disruptions: Jolts in market trends, general economic slowdowns, or entry by aggressive competitors disturb stability.
- Reputational Risks: Negative customer feedback, PR issues, or regulatory disputes harm a startup's image.
- Team-Related Crises: Factors such as internal conflicts, high attrition rates, or leadership changes can disrupt morale and productivity.

Handling a crisis well starts with acknowledging and assessing the situation. Recognizing the problem and understanding its impact is the first and most critical step. Denial or delay can exacerbate the situation, so facing the crisis head-on and getting the right information to assess its reach is important. Clarity helps founders to act fast and take decisive decisions that are very essential for a high-pressure situation. Developing a quick action plan to address the immediate concerns helps minimize disruption and sets the foundation for recovery.

Managing such crises is impossible without transparent communication. Keeping stakeholders-employees, investors, and customers informed gains trust and stops misinformation. Honest updates reassure everyone involved and keep everyone in sync during tricky times. Equally important is to use the strengths of your team. Task people according to their expertise and encourage people to work in all possible ways to bring in a united effort against the crisis. Consolidated approaches resolve issues effectively and reinforce morale.

The final move is adopting a solution-oriented mindset. That means instead of what went wrong, the decisive step would be towards fixing the problem. This is a forward-looking way, which instils confidence in the team and keeps the business operating in a positive trend. Crises will come; it's a natural component of crises, but with the right strategies—understanding the situation, acting quickly, communicating transparently, and keeping solutions at the centre of activity—startups can find their way around even the toughest roads to emerge stronger on the other side.

Practical Tips for Crisis Management:

- Develop a Crisis Plan Ahead of Time: Identify areas that may be likely to cause crises and prepare a plan that clearly outlines the key steps, roles, and responsibilities for all the different scenarios.
- Maintain Financial Buffers: Maintain an emergency fund to help deal with unexpected financial shocks.
- Build a Reliable Network: Advisors, mentors, or peers may be able to bring insights and support during times of crisis.
- Practice Crisis Drills: Simulate potential crisis scenarios to test the preparedness and then fine-tune strategies.
- Stay Calm and Lead the Way: A calm leader can calm the team's nerves and keep their spirits up during troublesome times.

Zomato, a leading Indian food delivery platform, faced a major crisis during the COVID-19 pandemic when lockdowns disrupted its core operations. Instead of panicking, Zomato quickly pivoted its business model by introducing "Zomato Market," a grocery delivery service that leveraged its existing delivery network. The company also maintained transparent communication with its employees and customers, ensuring trust and loyalty. This quick adaptation helped Zomato not only survive the crisis but move further up the market.

A crisis tests a startup's resilience and adaptability. Preparation well in advance, solution focus, and leading with confidence help even in the toughest challenges to emerge stronger. A crisis can become an opportunity to innovate, rebuild, and grow - if handled wisely.

CHAPTER TEN

Reaching the Destination: Long-Term Success and Exit Strategies

The journey of a startup doesn't end with survival or achieving initial milestones—it's about transitioning into a sustainable, impactful, and adaptable business that thrives over time. Long-term success requires more than growth; it demands a vision for the future, an innovative mindset, and the ability to evolve in dynamic markets. In this stage of the entrepreneurial journey, founders are challenged to move beyond profits and create lasting value, not just for themselves but also for customers, employees, and society.

True success is found in the science of striking a balance between ambition and sustainability. A successful business enterprise is always reinventing itself, changing to meet the trend and keeping relevance in the competitive scenario. Examples such as Amul, which changed the face of the dairy industry in India, exemplify how businesses can be innovative and stay true to their values. This leads to longevity based on a bedrock of resilience, improvement, and customer requirements.

As businesses mature, planning for the future is inevitable. Exit strategies are not only about monetary gain; they are about a shift in leadership, direction, and even potential for growth. Exit strategies can unlock new opportunities for the company while giving founders time to focus on new challenges or personal goals. Such exits, for instance, paved the way for significant expansions and recognition of Indian startups like BigBasket, giving proof that an exit may not mean an end but a transformative new chapter.

This chapter dives into what it takes to reach the pinnacle of entrepreneurial success, guiding readers on sustaining growth, preparing for exits, and building legacies. It challenges entrepreneurs to think boldly, act strategically, and dream of a future where their business not only survives but thrives and inspires for generations to come.

Sustaining Growth and Innovation

These two engines, sustaining growth and fostering innovation, drive businesses toward long-term success. Growth lets the company expand its reach, impact, and profitability, while innovation will help it stay competitive and relevant in a fast-changing world. Together, they form a cycle of advancement that will not only strengthen the company but also benefit its customers, employees, and society.

For businesses, sustained growth is not just scaling revenue; it is about creating a long-term impact and staying ahead of the curve. Growth provides opportunities for diversification, untapped markets, and attracting talent. Without innovation, growth can plateau, leaving businesses vulnerable to competitors and market shifts. Innovation ensures adaptability, opens doors to new possibilities, and solves real-world problems.

From a societal perspective, innovation-driven growth represents a source of employment, new technological advancements, and solutions to everyday problems. Businesses that embrace these principles often redefine industries, push boundaries, and contribute to a better world.

Infosys, one of India's pioneering IT companies, is a fine example of how growth and innovation can be interlinked. When Infosys was still in its nascent stage, the company had to compete with established global firms. In order to stand out from the crowd, they introduced the Global Delivery Model, which revolutionized the IT outsourcing industry by making services faster, more scalable, and cost-efficient. This innovation not only drove Infosys' growth but also set a new industry standard.

Even after decades, Infosys remains at the top of its game by always staying ahead in technology. Its investments in AI, digital transformation, and sustainability initiatives demonstrate how constant innovation keeps a business relevant. Besides profits, Infosys has made a difference in society through its Foundation, focusing on education and healthcare, showing that real growth is much more than financial success.

Steps to Sustain Growth and Innovation:

- Stay Customer-Focused: Always listen to customer feedback to anticipate evolving needs. Companies that prioritize their customers remain resilient and adaptive.
- Invest in R&D: Dedicate resources to exploring creative solutions and experimenting with bold ideas.

- Encourage Collaboration: Foster a culture where employees are motivated to share new ideas, take risks, and innovate.
- Adopt Emerging Technologies: Leverage tools like AI, IoT, and automation to optimize operations and create cutting-edge offerings.

Growth and innovation are not destinations but a journey, full-time attention, flexibility, and a mindset to change. For startups, these are the basis of long-term success. Through constant refinement of strategy and exploration of new possibilities, a startup would be sure to survive and thrive in such challenges. True growth is in the ability to innovate constantly, meeting the changing desires of the market and the customer.

Besides guaranteeing the longevity of the business, growth, and innovation are meant to shape the future of industries and have a wider influence on society. For this reason, a company that leads with its innovation builds up a reputation for thinking ahead, and for being resilient, thus attracting the right customers, investors, and top talent. The Infosys saga from being a small startup to being a global leader is enough proof that with some innovative strategy and persistence, even the toughest obstacles can be turned into opportunities.

For an entrepreneur, the lesson is simple: set the pace; don't just follow the market. The mantra of adapting ought to be embraced by a given startup, and it will not only get through trying times but win a legacy in its field and beyond.

Planning for the Future: Exit Strategies and Acquisitions

For any entrepreneur, the path to success does not just end with growth but extends into the future, where planning for the next stage becomes equally important. Exit strategies and acquisitions are critical tools that help entrepreneurs realize the value of their hard work while paving the way for future growth. An exit strategy involves planning how to step away from your business, be it selling it, merging with another company, or taking it public. It's not a question of cashing out but rather strategically positioning the company for long-term success, allowing it to continue growing and prospering even after the founder has exited.

Knowing when and how to exit is important. The right exit strategy enables entrepreneurs to unlock value either through the sale, which is profitable; an acquisition that increases prospects for the business; or a new opportunity that would not be accessible otherwise. Strategic acquisitions can help startups scale up very fast; tap into new markets; and increase competitive advantages. Acquisitions would often bring more than just financial prosperity for today's startups; acquisitions can provide new capabilities, technologies, and customer bases that are good drivers for future success.

The standout example of strategic acquisition would be the acquisition of WhatsApp by Facebook in 2014. WhatsApp is a messaging application founded by Jan Koum and Brian Acton. It had gained 600 million users at the time of acquisition. At that time, WhatsApp was an incredibly popular application with no clear model for revenue generation. What Facebook saw was the sheer number of users and technology capability. By acquiring WhatsApp for $19 billion, Facebook not only eliminated a potential competitor but also merged a powerful communication tool into its portfolio to strengthen its position in the mobile messaging space.

With the acquisition, Facebook could scale its offer and expand into various other products that had been built on its network, further opening communication lines on each of its platforms.

Additionally, Facebook escaped the dangers of losing market share due to WhatsApp and other technologies being developed around the globe. The purchase was, therefore, for Koum and Acton a surety for attaining financial success while being able to guarantee long-term stability in terms of its growth and continuation under Facebook's wing.

This acquisition is proof of the enormous value that can be extracted from an exit strategy and acquisition, well executed. Entrepreneurs can use these tools to grow beyond their original vision, meet financial goals, and create opportunities for their businesses to thrive in new ways.

Building a Legacy: Social Responsibility and Impact

Success in entrepreneurship is not only about profits or market share but also about the legacy left behind. Social responsibility is the bridge between business success and societal impact. It reflects a company's commitment to ethical practices, sustainability, and community welfare. For startups, embedding social responsibility into their DNA isn't just a moral obligation—it's a strategic move that builds trust, loyalty, and long-term value.

As startups grow, so does their ability to create meaningful change. Businesses hold unique power in addressing pressing social and environmental challenges, extending the impact far beyond immediate stakeholders. Prioritizing social responsibility benefits society but also strengthens the business itself. A socially responsible company earns customer loyalty by aligning with modern consumers' values; many customers today choose brands that contribute to the greater good. In addition, initiatives that foster employee engagement bring pride to the employees and increase morale and productivity. The businesses also become strong brands with a good reputation, earning respect and credibility as ethical and innovative leaders in their respective industries. Ultimately, social responsibility is not about doing good; it is about how the business will sustain itself over the long term, develop trust, and leave a lasting legacy to benefit all stakeholders while securing the planet's future.

The influential impact of socially responsible businesses cuts across communities and industries, as their influence can be profound by fostering sustainability, supporting underprivileged communities, or being inclusionists. Investing in these areas will not only help startups raise society but also build strong business resilience to adequately face the future.

Few companies exemplify the spirit of social responsibility as profoundly as the Tata Group, which has been a driving force in India's progress while marking its footprint worldwide. Tata's commitment to blending business excellence with societal development established a benchmark corporate social responsibility aimed to meet, showing how companies may lead with purpose and compassion.

Tata Steel's Model Village Development Program has revived the rural economy by building schools, health centres, and other critical infrastructure in India. Tata Trusts has dealt with systemic issues like poverty, malnutrition, and lack of education, raising millions. Programs that deal with women empowerment and sustainable energy further reveal Tata's efforts toward a better future for everyone.

Beyond India, Tata's work in Africa showcases its global spread. Tata International has partnered with universities to improve education, established e-learning centres, and imparted industry-specific training in hospitality and leather. Tata Chemicals Magadi has supported an HIV clinic in Nkurumani. Tata's Operation Smile missions have given free cleft lip and palate surgeries to transform thousands of lives. Tying up with the Red Cross further shows Tata's commitment to causes for humanity.

Tata's unparalleled efforts prove that success is not just about profits but about leaving a legacy of positive change. Entrepreneurs and businesses worldwide can learn from Tata's journey, understanding that true leadership lies in serving both people and the planet.

Lessons from Successful Entrepreneurs

Every successful entrepreneur carries a treasure trove of lessons gained in his or her journey of navigating untrodden territories, embracing failures, and redrafting industries. These lessons serve to illuminate the path for aspiring entrepreneurs into lessons on perseverance, innovation, and leadership. In the following pages, explore five incredible journeys: from uncharted territories with the entrepreneurs Anupam Mittal, Elon Musk, Mark Zuckerberg, Melanie Perkins, and Kiran Mazumdar-Shaw—and unearth some of the best learnings that can guide the next generation of change-makers.

Anupam Mittal: Founder of Shaadi.com

Anupam Mittal's journey started at a time when online matchmaking was considered an improbable concept in India's traditional society. Not deterred by scepticism, he recognized the potential of the internet and its power to transform conventional practices. Mittal adapted Shaadi.com to meet the evolving needs of Indian families, proving that understanding cultural nuances and adapting to societal changes are critical for success. His persistence in manoeuvring challenges such as low internet penetration and societal resistance reminds about the importance of patience and long-term vision.

Lesson: Success lies in identifying untapped markets and evolving your business to align with cultural and technological shifts.

Elon Musk: CEO of Tesla and SpaceX

Few entrepreneurs embody audacity and vision like Elon Musk. From pioneering electric vehicles with Tesla to revolutionizing space exploration with SpaceX, Musk has consistently tried to solve large-scale global problems. His journey wasn't easy: Tesla faced near-bankruptcy, while several rockets failed at SpaceX. Still, Musk's steady dedication to innovation and rallying his teams around aggressive objectives turned what could have easily been disasters into breathtaking triumphs. His approach emphasizes that resilience coupled with bold decisions can tackle anything even when it seems quite impossible.

Lesson: Dream big, take calculated risks, and never let temporary setbacks deter your vision for solving global problems.

Mark Zuckerberg: CEO of Meta (Facebook)

Mark Zuckerberg's ascend with Facebook is now Meta-is an exemplification of grasping what users want and creating platforms that connect people. Transforming the college networking site into a global communication platform is a testament to Zuckerberg's forward-looking sensibility. His pivot to virtual reality and the metaverse has shown the direction of staying ahead in industry trends. It is a story of innovation; a journey emphasizing the importance of constant iteration and change for long-term success.

Lesson: Prioritize user needs, evolve your product, and anticipate future trends to remain relevant and competitive.

Melanie Perkins: Co-Founder and CEO of Canva

Melanie Perkins' story is one of perseverance and simplicity. Canva, her design platform, has disrupted the graphic design industry by bringing professional tools to everyone's desk, regardless of their skill level. She began with an idea to simplify design and had to be rejected by hundreds of investors before she could get the funding. Her journey emphasizes the power of understanding pain points and simplifying complex problems to create solutions that resonate globally. In the story, Perkins' determination illustrates how belief in one's vision, combined with constant refinements, can lead to wonderful success.

Lesson: Solve universal problems with simple, user-friendly solutions, and never lose faith in your idea, even in the face of rejection.

Kiran Mazumdar-Shaw: Founder of Biocon

Kiran Mazumdar-Shaw's story at the helm of India's biopharmaceutical major Biocon is proof that all barriers can be crossed with purposeful impact. When she first took to her mission of making health more affordable, not just a few raised sceptical voices in this male bastion; she persevered to deliver innovation with a social purpose toward transforming access to medicines and healthcare globally. Shaw's story exemplifies a corporate strategy that integrates business with a purposeful cause, and how companies can attain profitability while improving society.

Lesson: Break barriers, stay purpose-driven, and create solutions that address real societal needs, all while maintaining a commitment to innovation.

Key Lessons from These Icons:

- Adapt to Cultural and Market Changes (Anupam Mittal): Anupam Mittal's journey with Shaadi.com epitomizes the importance of understanding cultural dynamics and adapting to shifting societal trends. He took a traditionally offline, family-driven matchmaking process and transformed it into a trusted online platform embracing India's evolving digital landscape. The lesson here is clear: Stay attuned to the cultural and market shifts, innovate accordingly, and don't shy away from challenging conventional norms.
- Embracing Bold Visions and Taking Risks (Elon Musk): Elon Musk's ventures, such as Tesla and SpaceX, are examples of how calculated risks can be powerful in pushing boundaries and solving global problems. His steadfast commitment to electric vehicles and reusable rockets, even after setbacks, speaks to the value of thinking big and staying resilient. Entrepreneurs must dream boldly, for the greatest achievements often come from the riskiest endeavours.
- Focus on Users and Stay Ahead of Trends (Mark Zuckerberg): Mark Zuckerberg's relentless focus on user experience has been the driving force behind Facebook (now Meta)'s evolution into a global social and technological powerhouse. From enabling global connectivity to pioneering the metaverse, Zuckerberg teaches entrepreneurs to always prioritize user needs while anticipating future technological trends. Building for today while preparing for tomorrow ensures your business remains relevant and competitive.
- Simplify the difficult problems, and follow through (Melanie Perkins): Melanie Perkins shook up the design world with Canva by making professional graphic design accessible to everyone. Her story is a reminder that solving universal pain points in an accessible way can lead to massive success. She had faced

numerous investor rejections early on, but she did not give up on her vision. The takeaway is to keep solutions simple, and user-friendly, and never let initial setbacks deter your belief in your idea.

- Drive Social Impact with Purpose (Kiran Mazumdar-Shaw): Kiran Mazumdar-Shaw's creation of Biocon highlights the significance of combining innovation with a mission-driven approach. She broke barriers in the male-dominated biotech industry and focused on producing affordable medicines, making healthcare accessible to millions. Entrepreneurs can learn to balance profitability with social good, proving that businesses can be both impactful and commercially successful.

These entrepreneurs have built spectacular businesses, reshaped entire industries, and created long-lasting legacies. Their journeys show that success is a combination of vision, resilience, adaptability, and relentless focus on solving meaningful problems, what aspiring entrepreneurs can learn from them is the set of tools and mindset to face all challenges and build their way to success.

Mastering the Fundamentals: Skills That Define Entrepreneurial Success

Entrepreneurship is passion, innovation, and resilience. Still, the best ideas and will in the world are not enough to guarantee success on their own. The real game-changers are the skills you acquire and master along the way.

Every entrepreneur has a unique path, but some skills stand the test of time. These essential skills are the foundation of great leadership, right decision-making, and sustainable growth. They empower entrepreneurs to respond to challenges, seize opportunities, and build lasting ventures.

In this section, we discuss the top ten most critical skills every entrepreneur should develop. These are not just characteristics of successful founders; they're the toolkit for navigating business complexities, managing teams, and delivering value to customers and society.

The Art of Selling: Convincing with Confidence

Selling is more than just making someone want to buy something from you. It's about creating an offer that resonates with the needs and emotions relevant to your target audience. In other words, it's the art of connecting personally, showing them where the pain is, and how your product or service helps eliminate that problem or brings value to their lives. Whether you're pitching to customers, negotiating with investors, or inspiring employees, selling is a critical skill that underpins the growth and survival of any business.

Sales are the fuel that keeps a business running. A brilliant product or service won't work without a compelling narrative driving adoption. Entrepreneurs must sell their vision to get funding, build partnerships, and gain customer trust. Selling is not just closing deals; it's building long-term relationships that help with loyalty and growth.

It leads to missed opportunities and even the most innovative ideas remaining unrealized. With this skill, a great entrepreneur can gain market traction not only in his vision but also inspire belief in his vision. That is why it is said that an entrepreneur is always selling—selling their ideas, their products, their services.

Practical Tips:

- Master the Art of Storytelling: Transform your pitch into a relatable and emotionally engaging story. Use real-life examples or customer experiences to illustrate how your product solves a problem. A compelling narrative can make your pitch memorable, leaving a lasting impression on your audience. For example, instead of listing features, share how a customer's life was transformed after using your service.
- Focus on Active Listening: The great salesperson talks less and listens more. Through proper questions, learn the customer's needs, preferences, and concerns to fine-tune your pitch by directly tackling their pain points. It is when you listen that you get to trust the individual or even let them feel you care to solve his or her problem.
- Understand Your Product and Competitors Inside Out: Confidence comes from knowledge. Be an expert on your product or service and how it compares to competitors. Highlight your unique selling points (USPs) clearly and explain why your solution is the best choice. This level of preparation

builds credibility and helps handle objections effectively during conversations.

Stress and Time Management: Balancing the Load

Two of the best supports for an entrepreneur's smooth operation are managing stress and time. When it comes to staying organized with proper time usage, you always know whether you can answer to a fast-paced environment in a startup. Normally, a startup is normally disorderly as it comes with changing priorities and deadlines due to resource deficiencies. Handling such dynamics without getting burnt out forms an ability every entrepreneur has to master.

Uncontrolled stress will siphon creativity from a person's mind, diminish the level of his productivity, and even hamper his ability in making decisions. An entrepreneur finds himself stretched thin by having to deal with multiple responsibilities most of the time, which always leads to poor work performances and health conditions. Also, the best utilization of time increases proficiency and gives a person the mental space to think and innovate strategically. Learning to manage stress and time enables entrepreneurs to manage resilience, stay focused, and create a sustainable work life that will impel long-term success.

A startup thrives if its founder succeeds. If one is organized, focused, and can keep calm in the face of pressure, then that rubs off on the team and business operations. Time and stress management are not just individual skills but leadership qualities that dictate the tone for the rest of the company.

Practical Tips:

- Break down tasks and prioritize with precision: Start each day with a clear plan. Use tools like the Eisenhower Matrix to sort tasks by urgency and importance. Focus on high-priority tasks first, and delegate or schedule fewer pressing ones for later. This ensures that you're tackling what matters most without being overwhelmed by the entire workload.
- Adopt Mindfulness Techniques and Physical Activities: Regular mindfulness practices, such as meditation or deep breathing exercises, help manage stress by grounding your mind and enhancing clarity. Complement this with physical activities like yoga or running, which are proven stress-busters and energy boosters. A healthy mind and body are your best assets in a demanding entrepreneurial journey.
- Leverage Technology for Efficiency: Tools like Trello, Asana, or Notion can organize workflows by breaking down tasks, setting deadlines, and showing progress. Automate as much as possible, with the help of tools like Zapier or Slack integrations, in order to free up time for strategic activities.

Financial Literacy: Controlling the Numbers

Financial literacy is the knowledge to understand and manage the financial heartbeat of your startup. It's knowing where your money comes from, where it goes, and how to make it work smarter for your business. From budget creation to cash flow tracking and profit margins, financial literacy equips entrepreneurs to make sound decisions that drive sustainable growth. In such a situation, you may not be a wizard of finance, but your understanding of the finances can give you that clear path to guide your startup toward success.

It's like driving a car with no idea of the quantity of fuel that is left in the tank. It is hazardous and uncertain and would eventually turn out to be very negative. Startups mostly run on tight budgets, with every rupee playing an important role. The companies are likely to squander resources—either overspend, under-invest, or go bankrupt without the help of an effective financial plan.

Financial literacy prevents disasters and builds credibility. That confidence of speaking about your financial projections before investors or members of your team goes a long way in earning trust and control. It would also give you an idea of what you should be cutting on non-essential expenses and opportunities for growth. Not just living, but also setting the foundation for sustainable success.

Practical Tips:

- Learn the Basics with Focus: Understanding financial statements such as profit and loss, balance sheets, and cash flow statements may sound scary, but it's easy. You can learn to break down these basics from free resources on platforms such as YouTube or Coursera.
- Use Smart Financial Tools: Why should everything be done manually when there are tools like QuickBooks or Zoho Books to ease bookkeeping and expense tracking. These tools will also help you keep track of cash flow, generate reports, and even manage taxes with minimal effort.
- Find a Mentor or Join a Startup Group: Sometimes reach out to experienced entrepreneurs or financial advisors who can lead you through the tricky parts. Peer learning is equally strong, and join those communities where you can learn other strategies and best practices that others have adopted.

Decision-Making: Turning Uncertainty into Action

Entrepreneurship is fundamentally a matter of decision-making. It is the ability to navigate uncertainty and make choices that will shape the future of your startup. Whether it is hiring the right talent, launching a new product, allocating resources, or pivoting strategies, entrepreneurs face critical decisions every day. What makes all the difference is the ability to weigh out situations quickly and act confidently with incomplete information.

In the startup world, where things happen quickly, sometimes a delay or lack of decision can be worse than a wrong decision. Hesitation may cost an opportunity; rash decisions may lead to costly mistakes. Entrepreneurs need to be analytical enough to make judgments about the risks involved and bold enough to take decisive action. A good decision-making process helps drive progress and builds confidence and trust with investors, employees, and customers alike.

Good decisions give a path to sustainable growth, while bad ones offer valuable learning. The key is having a decision framework that works to bring uncertainty into momentum. Within the right state of mind, every decision builds on others to lead towards lasting success.

Practical Tips:

- Balance data with instinct: Gather relevant data to guide your choices, but don't ignore your intuition. For example, data can show market trends, but your instinct may point you toward unexplored opportunities. When combined, this balance leads to well-rounded decisions.
- Apply Decision-Making Frameworks: Structured frameworks

such as pros-and-cons lists, cost-benefit analyses, or SWOT analysis (Strengths, Weaknesses, Opportunities, Threats) will guide and organize your thoughts. They ensure that you analyse options objectively, minimizing the risk of making biased or emotion-driven decisions.

- Draw on Experience: Treat every decision as an opportunity to learn. Review past choices regularly and identify what worked, what didn't, and why. This reflection not only sharpens your judgment but also builds a repository of lessons to guide future decisions.

Networking: Building Bridges to Opportunities

Networking is a competency that focuses on developing and nurturing the significant relationships that create opportunities for cooperation, mentorship, and financial resources. It is more than collecting business cards; it means developing connections that support mutual development. In the entrepreneurial world, a good network can be what separates a missed opportunity from a major breakthrough. This is the only way for a startup to open up more doors for itself, whether it is seeking an appropriate investor, securing a strategic alliance, or learning from an experienced mentor.

Business success often depends on "who you know." Networking provides opportunities that might not be advertised or even seeable. Investors are more likely to fund entrepreneurs when they can see them-or when they were referred to an entrepreneur by a respected colleague. Similarly, partnerships and mentorships usually arise from meaningful relationships. It requires a strong network, which can grow your startup overnight and put you in a position to be that name people trust in the industry.

It's not only about personal gains but also about contribution to your community. From sharing insights to supporting peers and generating win-win collaborations, it will make you a very reliable and resourceful entrepreneur in the long run.

Practical Tips:

- Attend the right events: Engage in online and offline events such as industry conferences, startup meetups, and webinars. Target gatherings relevant to your field or where potential collaborators and investors are likely to be. Platforms like LinkedIn and Meetup are the best tools for discovering opportunities.
- Follow up and remain engaged: Send a personalized message or email to that person after you connect. Keep them engaged with constant activity, whether it is sharing industry insights, congratulating them on achievements, or checking in. Building relationships takes time.
- Offer Value First: Networking is a two-way street. Take a genuine interest in the needs and goals of your connections and be there to help, whether that is through advice, an introduction, or just access to resources. Generosity with your network usually brings about stronger, more fruitful connections.

Creative Problem-Solving: Thinking Outside the Box

Creative problem-solving is solving a problem by using new and unusual approaches rather than the only accepted methods. With a smart and resourceful mindset, an insurmountable problem might be framed as an opportunity. Such is the characteristic that characterizes many successful entrepreneurs in a startup's unpredictable climate of unexpected challenges. Creative problem-solving is definitely not a reaction to trouble but a proactive approach intended to promote growth and innovation.

Startups are the ones that function under uncertainty, where the resource scarcity, intense competition, and volatile markets characterize such environments. Under such conditions, innovation becomes a necessary tool for entrepreneurs because traditional tools cannot be used here; instead, innovation can ensure that startups survive turmoil but, at the same time, create new space for differentiation and success. For most startups, innovation provides a leading edge in its respective market through cost-effective marketing campaigns to redesigning product attributes.

Creative problem-solving also drives innovation, helping businesses stay relevant in fast-changing industries. It fosters a culture of experimentation, encouraging teams to push boundaries and embrace new possibilities.

Practical Tips:

- Embrace Brainstorming: Create an environment where you and your team can generate multiple ideas for addressing your problems. Techniques like "mind-mapping" or structured brainstorming encourage free-flowing ideas. Go for quantity, then refine into quality later.
- Experiment Fearlessly: Unconventional methods can lead to breakthroughs. Don't hesitate to test new strategies or technologies, even if they seem risky at first. For instance, small-scale pilot projects or A/B testing can provide insights without massive upfront commitments.
- Use Root Cause Analysis Tools Like "The Five Whys": When a problem arises, dig deep by asking "Why?" many times. This structured approach uncovers the underlying issues, enabling you to address the root cause rather than surface symptoms. For example, a drop in sales might not be because of poor marketing but because of an unmet customer need that wasn't identified

before.

Adaptability: Staying Ahead of Change

Adaptability is being able to adjust quickly and effectively to changes within the market, technology, or business environment. In the unpredictable world of startups, this is a key trait for survival and growth. It allows an entrepreneur to respond to obstacles, pivot when necessary, and seize new opportunities that emerge from change. To be adaptable does not mean abandoning a vision; it means being flexible in approach to achieve a vision.

The landscape of startups is constantly changing with fast-paced technological progress, changing consumer preferences, and ups and downs in the economy. Entrepreneurs who resist change are bound to be left behind, whereas those embracing change have a competitive advantage. Resilience also comes through adaptability, which allows businesses to move through the shocks that might be caused by new competitors, new regulations, or unexpected global events like a pandemic.

It's being flexible that guarantees the survival of your startup. Being flexible helps foster innovation. Companies that adapt are most likely to find new ways of serving their customers, enter new markets, and improve operations that position them for long-term success.

Practical Tips:

- Stay Informed About Industry Trends: Keep a pulse on your industry through reading reports, attending webinars, and networking with peers. This keeps you informed so that you can anticipate the changes rather than react to them. For instance, those startups that adopted remote work early were thriving during the global disruptions.

- Encourage Feedback from Team and Customers: Honest and regular feedback is your compass. Talk regularly to your team and know where to focus and how to improve; communicate with your customers to understand them and thus ensure your offers remain relevant. Agile start-ups live by this continuous feedback and iteration loop.
- Be Prepared to Pivot: Review your business model, strategies, or product offerings as needed. Pivoting is not a failure but a strategic move to align with changing circumstances. For example, many startups started by solving one problem but ended up succeeding by pivoting to another more promising opportunity.

Leadership: Inspiring and Guiding Teams

An aspect of a successful startup goes beyond just managing tasks - it's influencing, inspiring, and guiding toward shared vision, leaders have to encourage a sense of purpose and in a harmoniously balanced group of people with diverse talent and experiences. It breeds confidence and builds strength in its members in the simplest but most indispensable way, particularly at an uncertain time at which a high-stakes environment is that of a startup.

Startups gather the best of different people and experiences to achieve great things, often under significant constraints. Without great leadership, even the best team will seem lost and directionless without a clear purpose. It is the leader who gets everyone working towards a specific goal, who makes things work as a team and keeps morale up, no matter what happens. Leadership inspires trust not only within your team but also among investors, partners, and even customers. It builds that foundation of confidence that powers long-term success.

Practical Tips:

- Set a Clear and Compelling Vision: Describe where your startup is headed and why it matters. A well-articulated vision is a guiding star for your team, keeping them motivated and aligned. Share your vision regularly to remind your team of the bigger picture, especially in difficult phases.
- Lead by Example: Actions speak louder than words. Show the values you expect your team to embrace-perseverance, empathy, or excellence. If you want your team to work hard, then you have to work hard. When leaders act like what they preach, then that's where respect and loyalty start coming from their teams.
- Set an environment of trust and inclusiveness: A team that feels trusted and included performs better. Encourage open communication, listen to feedback, and value diverse perspectives. When people feel respected and heard, they're more likely to contribute their best ideas and efforts toward the startup's success.

Customer-Centric Thinking: Putting Customers at the Heart of Your Startup

Customer-centric thinking is a process of organizing and running a business by primarily keeping in mind the needs of the customer. This thinking, therefore, includes an extensive knowledge of the customer's needs, wants, and pain points concerning the customer's preferences so that the products, services, and interactions may be personalized to solve problems and exceed expectations. Being skilful with this ensures that every decision-making, whether in product development, marketing, or also in customer service, is based on the objective of customer value creation.

In today's competitive landscape, customers have more power than ever. They have endless choices and loyalty has to be earned. Startups embracing customer-centric thinking are not only able to satisfy their customers but also build brand advocates that amplify their message. Customer-centricity ensures stronger retention, better feedback loops, and long-term profitability. In simple words, businesses that prioritize their customers thrive, while those that don't struggle to stay relevant.

Organizations such as Amazon and Zappos are lauded for their customer-centric approaches, which demonstrates that the customer is not just an ethical consideration but also a smart business move.

Practical Tips:

- Invest in Deep Customer Understanding: It's not only demographics that should be known; rather, it's their behaviours, motivations, and challenges. Conduct regular surveys, interviews, and focus groups. Tools like Google Analytics and Heatmaps provide data-driven insights into how customers interact with your offerings, so you can make informed decisions.
- Design Every Interaction with Empathy: View your business from the customer's perspective. Simplify your website, provide fast responses, and ensure that your product delivers on its promises. A seamless empathetic experience creates lasting impressions and wins loyalty.
- Develop a Culture of Continuous Feedback: Provide opportunities for customers to be heard through surveys, reviews, or direct channels. And then act on them. Showing customers that your actions are a result of their opinions builds

trust and relationships.

Emotional Resilience: Staying Strong Through Tough Times

The ability to bounce back from setbacks, adjust to challenges, and press forward with unwavering determination. For entrepreneurs, this quality is more than just skill; it is a crucial survival mechanism. Entrepreneurs face many setbacks: pitches that fail, money problems, product failures, and unexpected market shifts. Emotional resilience means being able to ride out such choppy waters without losing concentration or drive. You can make obstacles stepping stones to success in the future.

Entrepreneurship is highly uncertain and risky. Without resilience, challenges may seem insurmountable, and entrepreneurs may experience burnout or abandonment. Those who have resilience view setbacks as temporary and controllable rather than overwhelming. They do not view failures as definitive conclusions but as important lessons that improve their strategies and promote their development.

Emotional resilience makes teams, investors, and stakeholders rise to the occasion. A composed leader who is focused during bad times will definitely boost the morale and create trust, so everyone will be aligned in the vision of the startup.

Practical Tips:

- Reframe Failures as Opportunities to Learn: Change your perspective on failure. Instead of viewing it as a dead end, see it as a chance to analyse what went wrong and how to improve. Many successful entrepreneurs, like Ratan Tata, credit their failures for teaching them valuable lessons that shaped their successes.

- Build a Strong Support System: Surround yourself with mentors, peers, and friends who will be able to guide you, encourage you, and bring in perspective. Peer networks and entrepreneurial communities are fantastic for sharing challenges and getting insights from people who have faced the same hurdles.
- Maintain Your Mental and Physical Health: Do some self-care routines like mindfulness, meditation, or other physical activities that keep you in emotional balance. Time spent recharging will help you think more clearly, make better decisions, and avoid burnout when the situation gets more intense.

Note For Aspiring Entrepreneurs

Dear Aspiring Entrepreneur,

Congratulations on reaching the end of this book—but let me tell you, this is just the beginning of your journey. Starting up is not easy, and the path is often filled with challenges and doubt, both from others and sometimes from within. People may laugh at you, tell you that you're not capable, and insist you can't succeed. There will be moments when you find yourself standing alone, without a team or anyone to support you. But here's the truth: greatness is born in such moments of solitude and self-belief.

Be strong and unwavering in your resolve. Be dedicated to relentless growth-sharpening your skills and refining your idea until it evolves into something extraordinary. Every day is an opportunity to nurture your dream and bring it closer to reality. Hustle with purpose, and believe in your journey, even when others don't. If you have faith in your vision and trust in yourself, there are no limits to what you can accomplish.

Remember, success does not arrive overnight. Failure is the process, but it's also one of the stepping stones on the way forward. The only thing that is surely going to be there at every step is that every step will fill your arsenal with invaluable knowledge, hard-earned experience, and unshakable confidence that will not only prepare you for the future but will empower you to conquer it.

Challenges will come, but challenges are what shape you to become the champion you need to be. If sometimes you feel like you are going nowhere, take a break and think about why you started doing this. Believe in yourself-you can make something remarkable.

So, here's my final advice: if you are confident in your idea, don't let self-doubt or the opinions of others confuse or limit you. Trust your instincts, back your vision, and take that leap of faith.

You've got this. Now go out there and make the world believe in your dreams. You can do anything, champion.

With belief in you,
Your fellow aspiring Entrepreneur

www.ingramcontent.com/pod-product-compliance
Lightning Source LLC
LaVergne TN
LVHW041100150826
845673LV00007B/1862

* 9 7 9 8 8 9 7 2 4 2 3 7 5 *